LAY SERVANTS

as Christian Transformational Leaders

LAY SERVANTS

as Christian Transformational Leaders

PARTICIPANT'S BOOK

MARC BROWN, KATHY MERRY, *and* JOHN BRIGGS

DISCIPLESHIP
RESOURCES

ISBNs
978-0-88177-881-6 (print)
978-0-88177-882-3 (mobi)
978-0-88177-883-0 (ePub)
978-0-88177-884-7 (PDF downloadable leader's guide)

DR881

Dedications

Dedicated to the many church leaders who give of themselves for the cause of Christ in the world.—John Briggs

With gratitude for the transforming love of my wife Beverly; our daughter Ginny, her husband Bryan, their children Abby, Brady, and Frankie; and our son Adam, his wife Rachel, and their children, Ethan and Vivian.—Marc Brown

For my mother and father, Barbara and Ben Ashby. So thankful for their loving devotion to their family and their complete confidence in us.—Kathy Merry

CONTENTS

Contents

CHAPTER ONE

Defining Christian Transformational Leaders

The United Methodist Church has stated that "the mission of the Church is to make disciples of Jesus Christ for the transformation of the world."[1] If this goal is to be fulfilled, the church needs Christian transformational leaders. Where will these leaders come from and how will they lead movements of hope into a transformed vision of the world?

This book is designed to provide lay servants with scriptural foundations of Christian transformational leadership as well as organizational effectiveness principles. Our goal is to offer a framework for understanding how lay servants can be Christian transformational leaders in their congregations, workplaces, and the world.

Part One: Defining Christian Transformational Leaders

The journey of Christian transformational leaders begins with the story of Christian servanthood. Jesus tells the story of servanthood in each of the four gospels as he witnesses to the purpose of his life and ministry. One of these gospel accounts is found in Mark 10:35-45 as two of Jesus' disciples, James and John, ask Jesus to grant their request for seats of honor by Jesus' right and left sides in his glory.

> James and John, the sons of Zebedee, came forward to him and said to him, "Teacher, we want you to do for us whatever we ask of you." And he said to them, "What is it you want me to do for you?" And they said to him, "Grant us to sit, one at your right hand and one at your left, in your glory" (Mark 10:35-37).

Jesus responded to their request by telling them they did not know the magnitude of what they were asking. When the other disciples heard of the request that James and John had made of Jesus, they responded with indignation at these brothers' attempt to usurp leadership among the followers of Jesus. Responding to both the request by James and John and the indignation of the other disciples, Jesus taught about the difference between the world's understanding of power and leadership as contrasted with his understanding of power and leadership.

> "You know that among the Gentiles those whom they recognize as their rulers lord it over them, and their great ones are tyrants over them. But it is not so among you; but whoever wishes to become great among you must be your servant, and whoever wishes to be first among you must be slave of all. For the Son of Man came not to be served but to serve, and to give his life a ransom for many" (Mark 10:42b-45).

What was the difference between the leadership that James and John coveted and the leadership that Jesus embodied? Jesus differentiated between the leadership exhibited by power-craved rulers who lorded over their subjects and the servant leadership that he was incarnating as he sought to become the least of all.

When James and John asked to sit on Jesus' left and right sides, they hoped to rise to the top of the culture of power that defined their society. Their vision of power was short-sighted, as they sought to become *rulers of transformation* rather than *servants of transformation*. Jesus desired the transformation of the culture of power defined by their society, but he sought this transformation by living in the power of servant leadership. Rather than being a ruler who sought to be served, Jesus was a leader who sought to serve.

Rulers of Transformation—trust in their own vision of power as they instruct others toward a desired outcome.

Servants of Transformation—trust in Jesus' vision of power as they walk with others toward alignment with the cross.

The difference between the self-serving control of power that James and John craved and the power of servant leadership that Jesus modeled remains the single biggest barrier to transformation today. Too often, this barrier is manifested as people seek to exert control through the power of their leadership. Like James and

John, they live in the world's understanding of power by seeking to become rulers of transformation as they focus on the empowerment and advancement of their vision of leadership. This is not the vision of transformation that Jesus desired as he lived in the self-giving vulnerability of servanthood.

The ultimate sign of power in Jesus' day was the cross as used by the Roman Empire. This public method of execution was a sign of control that proclaimed the power of Rome and the powerlessness of those over whom Rome ruled.

The use of the cross as a sign of domination was perhaps most evident when Marcus Licinius Crassus, the Roman general and politician, defeated the slave revolt that was led by Spartacus in 72 BC. After the defeat of Spartacus, the remaining 6,000 participants of the slave rebellion were crucified on the road that led from Rome to Capua where the revolution had begun.

It was through the cross that Jesus' vision of servanthood would be comprehended in its fullest as he told James and John, "For the Son of Man came not to be served but to serve, and to give his life as a ransom for many" (Matthew 20:28).

For followers of Jesus to understand the true meaning of power in God's kingdom, they must understand the redeeming power of the cross as defined by Jesus. It is this contrasting vision of power that the apostle Paul wrote about in I Corinthians 1:18-31 as he invited the members of the Corinthian church to consider God's call upon their lives:

For the message about the cross is foolishness to those who are perishing, but to us who are being saved it is the power of God. For it is written,

"I will destroy the wisdom of the wise, and the discernment of the discerning I will thwart."

Where is the one who is wise? Where is the scribe? Where is the debater of this age? Has not God made foolish the wisdom of the world? For since, in the wisdom of God, the world did not know God through wisdom, God decided, through the foolishness of our proclamation, to save those who believe. For Jews demand signs and Greeks desire wisdom, but we proclaim Christ crucified, a stumbling block to Jews and foolishness to Gentiles, but to those who are the called, both Jews and Greeks, Christ the power of God and the wisdom of God. For God's foolishness is wiser than human wisdom, and God's weakness is stronger than human strength.

Consider your own call, brothers and sisters: not many of you were wise by human standards, not many were powerful, not many were of noble birth. But God chose what is foolish in the world to shame the wise; God chose what is weak in the world to shame the strong; God chose what is low and despised in the world, things that are not, to reduce to nothing things that are, so that no one might boast in the presence of God. He is the source of your life in Christ Jesus, who became for us wisdom from God, and righteousness and sanctification and redemption, in order that, as it is written, "Let the one who boasts, boast in the Lord" (I Corinthians 1:18-31).

The cross of Jesus Christ is where Jesus' vision of servant leadership is fully revealed and extended to people who answer Jesus' call upon their lives. Experiencing the redeeming power of the crucified and risen Christ, followers of Jesus are invited to trust in the vulnerable wisdom of God's kingdom that allowed Jesus to become the servant of all. While it may be tempting to think of servant leadership as a call that is confined to the church, in truth, it is a life call. The call to be a Christian transformational leader is not specific to *where* you lead but *how* you lead.

It is interesting to note how the concept of servant leadership has been adapted and applied in the business world. It is widely recognized throughout organizational effectiveness research and literature that leaders who put their personal and positional power to work in support of the people of their organization rather than in support of self are the most effective leaders. Following are observations from industry-leading authors on this subject:

"The servant-leader is servant first . . . It begins with the natural feeling that one wants to serve, to serve first. Then conscious choice brings one to aspire to lead. That person is sharply different from one who is leader first. . ."

(Robert K Greenleaf, founder of modern servant leadership movement, in his essay "The Servant as Leader")

"As we look ahead to the next century, leaders will be those who empower others."

(Bill Gates, business magnate, philanthropist, investor)

"Organizations exist to serve. Period. Leaders live to serve. Period."

(Tom Peters, writer on business management practices)

"Servant-leadership is more than a concept, it is a fact. Any great leader, by which I also mean an ethical leader of any group, will see herself or himself as a servant of that group and will act accordingly."

(M. Scott Peck, psychiatrist and best-selling author)

"Some of the greatest organizations today have turned themselves upside down. They have found that the old top-down pyramid style management structure doesn't work. Progressive companies have flipped the pyramid over. . ."

(Jim Collins, business consultant, author. and lecturer)

Viewing the Organization from a Servant-Leader Perspective

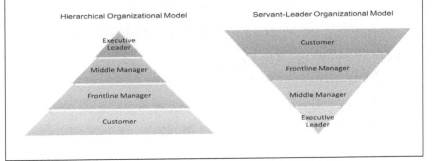

—— **Questions for Reflection and Discussion** ——

1. Why do you think the servant-leadership approach that Jesus modeled has become the most effective way to lead organizations in the business world?

2. How did Jesus' willing death on the cross transform the understanding of power through servant leadership?

3. What are ways that Christian transformational leaders can become vulnerable as they lead change?

Part Two: Leadership Responses to Current Reality

Followers of Jesus become Christian transformational leaders by pointing beyond themselves to the vision of God's kingdom. To understand how Christian transformational leaders point beyond themselves, it is important to define the role of leaders and how they respond to the current reality that defines the existence of an organization. Every current reality includes strengths, weaknesses, opportunities, and threats.

SWOT Analysis

The SWOT Analysis is a classic strategic planning tool that helps an organization plan for the future by analyzing the internal organization as well as the external factors that have an impact on the organization.

Strengths—internal positive attributes that contribute to the organization's identity and the reputation of success that is attributed to it by individuals, groups, or other organizations.

Weaknesses—internal challenges that have a negative impact on an organization as it seeks to fulfill its identified purpose or mission.

Opportunities—external factors and trends that are favorable to an organization as it seeks to fulfill its purpose.

Threats—external factors that create barriers for an organization as it seeks to fulfill its purpose.

Every current reality includes strengths, opportunities, weaknesses, and threats.

A congregation's current reality is defined by its strengths, weaknesses, opportunities, and threats. Factors such as its worshiping community, practice of spiritual disciplines, participation in small groups, giving habits of its members, age of congregants, congregational history, allocation of resources, condition of property, as well as the demographics of its surrounding community (gender, race, age, income levels, home ownership, population, etc.) affect its mission and ministry. Every congregation chooses how it will respond to its current reality. The congregation's leaders shape that response. Interpreting the strengths and weaknesses of an organization through the lens of opportunities and threats, the organization's leaders influence the behaviors and actions of the organization as they respond to current reality.

For the purpose of this book, we will define three of the ways leaders respond to the current reality of an organization: (1) present-tense leadership, (2) transformational leadership, and (3) Christian transformational leadership. Each way of responding is identified by particular characteristics.

Present Tense Leaders

- Respond to present condition
- Shape organization to comply

Transformational Leaders

- Respond to present and future condition
- Shape organization to desired outcome

Christian Transformational Leaders

- Respond to God's vision for the future as revealed through Jesus
- Shape organization to align with Jesus' call

Some leaders make a deliberate decision to adapt the ministry of a congregation or organization to the current reality it is experiencing. At other times, this choice is not a deliberate decision, but manifests itself as leaders focus on the present rather than the future. Instead of envisioning transformation, they maintain current patterns of ministry that have shaped the past and present identity of the congregation. In turn, the goal of preserving the present mission and ministry shapes the expectations of the leaders as they seek to maintain their congregational identity. The term we use to identify this leadership response to current reality is "present-tense leadership."

Sally is a "present-tense leader." She is organized and engaging. As soon as she accepts the role of church council chair, she sets about getting things organized. Sally views her role as maximizing the effectiveness of the current ministries of the congregation. She establishes meeting agendas, clarifies the role of the church council, and works with the staff-parish relations committee to get job descriptions in place. She has every committee set goals and talk about their progress toward those goals at every church council meeting. Many churches would perceive Sally to be an excellent church leader because of her efficient ability to organize the work of the church.

The goal of present-tense leaders is to maintain and order present congregational identity. Rather than seeking to lead transformational movements of hope into a future that is different from the past, they seek to lead movements of congregational satisfaction in the present. Allowing the expectations of the congregation's current identity to shape the expectations of their leadership, present-tense leaders focus on the present mission and ministry of a congregation.

The challenge that present-tense leaders face, however, is that their vision is bound by the congregation's current reality and identity. Guided by this vision, these leaders focus on maintaining a congregation's status quo as they help the congregation keep doing those ministries that have led to its current identity. Rather than resulting in congregational satisfaction, the vision of maintaining *current identity* in the midst of a changing *current reality* will lead to dissatisfaction as a congregation wanders in search of a relevant identity.

This search for relevant identity will lead a congregation to a decision point as it chooses whether it will *wander* in search of an identity or *intentionally seek* a new identity in response to its current reality. An intentional search for identity requires a different type of leader from a present-tense leader. This journey of searching for identity requires a transformational leader.

Transformational leaders shape present and future conditions in alignment with a desired outcome. Rather than simply responding to present conditions, they are able to align current reality with a desired outcome for a future that is different from the past. In this type of leadership, the identity of the transformational leader shapes the present and future identity of the organization.

> John is a transformational leader. He is articulate and sees the big picture. Once John accepts the role of church council chair, he begins talking about "who we want to be in five years." He has committees set goals according to that vision. He, too, organizes things well and has committees report on their progress toward their five-year goals.

Transformational leaders are guided by a vision that sees beyond the present. Rather than focusing on the *limitations* of a congregation's current reality, they envision the *possibilities* of a congregation's current reality. Accordingly, these envisioned possibilities serve as aligning points in helping a congregation to form or re-form its identity. Transformational leaders shape congregational identity by asking the right questions about vision, focus, opinions, ministries, and behaviors. The direction of their leadership moves a congregation beyond problem solving as they *ask right questions* that empower vulnerable responses to current reality and identity. Instead of current congregational reality shaping the identity and expectations of their leadership, transformational leaders shift the expectation of congregational response from maintaining the current reality to embracing a new reality. While the story of transformational leadership shapes the future narrative of a congregation's ministry, the story of congregational transformation must be connected to the larger biblical story of faith. For this story to be told, Christian transformational leadership is required.

Christian transformational leaders shape present and future conditions in alignment with Jesus' call to follow him. Christian transformational leaders align the life of a congregation with the future that God created and redeemed through Jesus. In this level of leadership, the identity of Jesus shapes the present and future identity of the congregation.

Sue is a Christian transformational leader. She is focused on Jesus' call for her church. Sue begins every meeting with a reminder that each church is called to love God with our whole hearts, minds, and souls and to love our neighbors as ourselves. She leads open discussions about what this call means to each member and to the church as a body. She asks questions about how well the people of the church know the community that surrounds the church. She asks how well the current committee structure promotes new ideas that align the church with Jesus' call. She works closely with the pastor and church leaders to re-envision the church's role in the community and world. She puts people and processes in place that will facilitate that vision. She consciously and constantly asks, "How does that activity/ministry help us love God and neighbor?"

Both transformational leaders and Christian transformational leaders share similar characteristics. They see beyond current reality. The difference is that transformational leaders lead a response to the future through their own vision. Christian transformational leaders respond to the current reality of an organization using Jesus' vision of servant leadership as their guide. Modeling Jesus' servant leadership, they respond to present conditions through faith in Jesus. Aligning both present and future opinions by nurturing people to become followers of Jesus, they lead movements of hope for a future that is different from the past and the present.

One of the clearest examples of Jesus' transformational leadership is found in the thirteenth chapter of the Gospel of John as Jesus washes his disciples' feet before his crucifixion. It is a powerful moment as Jesus assumes the function of a servant. It is a visible moment of transformed reality as Jesus, the teacher and Lord of the disciples, removes his outer clothing, wraps a towel around his waist, pours water into a basin, and begins to wash his disciples' feet, drying them with the towel that was wrapped around him. Seated at the table were the eleven disciples who would deny him and the one disciple, Judas, who would betray him. Jesus washed all of their feet, knowing that he would soon have authority exercised over him as he was condemned to the cross. In this knowledge, Jesus witnessed to a different understanding of transformational redemptive power as he completed his washing of the disciples' feet.

> After he had washed their feet, had put on his robe, and had returned to the table, he said to them, "Do you know what I have done to you? You call me Teacher and Lord—and

you are right, for that is what I am. So if I, your Lord and Teacher, have washed your feet, you also ought to wash one another's feet. For I have set you an example, that you also should do as I have done to you. Very truly, I tell you, servants are not greater than their master, nor are messengers greater than the one who sent them. If you know these things, you are blessed if you do them (John 13:12-17).

Washing the feet of his disciples, Jesus modeled the vision of Christian transformational leaders then and today. This mission is defined by the call to be transformed as followers of Jesus in the ministry of servanthood. In answering this call to leadership in our time, Christian transformational leaders realize the ministry of leadership needs to be more than a present-tense response to current reality. Assessing challenges and strengths, these leaders guide their organizations on a journey into a vision of a future that is beyond current reality. More than this, however, they understand that Christian transformational leaders guide their organizations into a vision of a future that is defined by the reality of a crucified and risen Lord who knelt to wash his disciples' feet. Rather than being transformational leaders who shape and influence change through their own power, Christian transformational leaders are shaped and influenced by Jesus' vision of power. Rather than leading by lording over others, they lead by witnessing to their Lord. They serve within the context of the culture of their day as Jesus served within the context of the culture of his day. They seek a vision of transformation that only Jesus makes possible as they lead by following Jesus.

—— **Questions for Reflection and Discussion** ——

1. Why is it important to define a congregation's current reality? How is a congregation's current reality defined?
2. What are the differences between present-tense leaders, transformational leaders, and Christian transformational leaders?
3. What lesson about Christian transformational leadership is Jesus teaching us in the foot-washing story of John 13? How can you model this lesson?

Part Three: Four Practices of Christian Transformational Leaders

Four practices empower Christian transformational leaders to lead by following Jesus: (1) enduring encouragement, (2) seeing beyond self-focused concerns, (3) asking right questions, and (4) leading by having the mind of Christ.

Practices that Empower Christian Transformational Leaders

1. Enduring Encouragement
2. Seeing Beyond Self-Focused Concerns
3. Asking Right Questions
4. Leading by Having the Mind of Christ

Enduring Encouragement: Without encouragement to change, organizations will seek to maintain current reality as shaped by present expectations. The term that describes the desire to maintain present organizational expectations is *equilibrium.* Defined as "a state in which opposing forces or influences are balanced," *equilibrium* is a desire to live within the known realities of current organizational dynamics rather than embrace unknown future challenges. Change requires organizations to lose their equilibrium as they risk living into a new future.

In a congregation, the loss of organizational balance often results in the shifting of power as congregational identity is defined, confessed, and redefined. It is a chaotic process as the values of current reality are measured against the values of a desired new future. Christian transformational leaders who are able to consistently remember, model, and encourage Jesus' teaching of servant leadership are required as they guide a congregation in aligning current realities with transformational possibilities.

Consider how Jesus modeled enduring encouragement as he interacted with his disciples in the tenth chapter of Mark and the thirteenth chapter of John. In both instances, Jesus remembered and encouraged the values of God's kingdom versus the values of the present culture. As already discussed, in the tenth chapter of Mark, Jesus contrasted the practice of rulers lording over their subjects with the values of servant leadership in God's kingdom. The thirteenth chapter of John shows Jesus washing his disciples' feet as he demonstrates a new understanding of what it means to be teacher and Lord. The disciples modeled enduring encouragement as the values of God's kingdom helped to shape the values of the early church. This practice still has the power to shape the values of today's church as it seeks to be a transformational agent in the world.

Barnabas was a Christian transformational leader who shaped the values of the early church by practicing enduring encouragement. The Book of Acts tells of how Barnabas received his name from the apostles after he sold a field he owned and gave the proceeds to the apostles.

> There was a Levite, a native of Cyprus, Joseph, to whom the apostles gave the name Barnabas (which means "son of encouragement"). He sold a field that belonged to him, then brought the money, and laid it at the apostles' feet (Acts 4:36-37).

This is not the only time Acts records Barnabas practicing enduring encouragement. Throughout the book of Acts, Barnabas is consistently present in key transitional moments as the identity and mission of the early church are defined. One of these key transitional moments is found in the ninth chapter of Acts as Barnabas stands with and for the most infamous persecutor of the early church, Saul (later to be named Paul), following Saul's conversion to the faith of Jesus Christ. The apostles were suspicious of Saul, but through Barnabas's encouragement, they were able to receive the person who had been the chief antagonist of the early church as a fellow follower of Jesus.

> When he had come to Jerusalem, he attempted to join the disciples; and they were all afraid of him, for they did not believe that he was a disciple. But Barnabas took him, brought him to the apostles, and described for them how on the road he had seen the Lord, who had spoken to him, and how in Damascus he had spoken boldly in the name of Jesus (Acts 9:26-27).

Barnabas was present at another key transitional moment when he was sent by the leaders of the church in Jerusalem to the church in Antioch to encourage new believers who were not Jewish. It was a defining moment of identity for the early church as the focus of its ministry was extended intentionally beyond Jerusalem. Evidence of this new identity is witnessed as disciples of Jesus are called Christians for the first time through the encouraging ministry of Barnabas.

> Now those who were scattered because of the persecution that took place over Stephen traveled as far as Phoenicia, Cyprus, and Antioch, and they spoke the word to no one except Jews. But among them were some men of Cyprus and Cyrene who, on coming to Antioch, spoke to the Hellenists also, proclaiming the Lord Jesus. The hand of the Lord was with them, and a great number became believers and turned to the Lord. News of this came to the ears of the church in Jerusalem, and they sent Barnabas to Antioch. When he came and saw the grace of God, he rejoiced, and he exhorted them all to remain faithful to the Lord with steadfast devotion; for he was a good man, full of the Holy Spirit and of faith. And a great many people were brought to the Lord. Then Barnabas went to Tarsus to look for Saul, and when he had found him, he brought him to Antioch. So it was that for an entire year they met with the church and taught a great many people, and it was in Antioch that the disciples were first called "Christians" (Acts 11:19-26).

Barnabas was present at the Council of Jerusalem in the fifteenth chapter of Acts when the equilibrium of the early church was affected as its identity was confessed, defined, and redefined by a formal statement of how Jewish believers in Jerusalem and Gentile believers in Antioch could be part of the same church. Practicing enduring encouragement, Barnabas was a faithful presence throughout the formative stages of the early church in Jerusalem as he gave the proceeds of the field he had sold, vouched for Saul before the apostles, witnessed to God's grace through his ministry with Saul in the church in Antioch, and participated in the Jerusalem Council. In each instance, Barnabas practiced being an enduring encourager as current realities were aligned with transformed possibilities.

Seeing Beyond Self-Focused Concerns: One of the realities of organizational life is that congregations can become stagnant in their ministry. Rather than being witnesses of the transformational power of Jesus, they can become witnesses of institutional protectionism as they seek to maintain the status quo. The language of mission is often replaced by the weight of organizational maintenance. Alignment to purpose can grow out of focus as vision turns inward. Connection with the community can be lost through self-focused concerns. The result of this direction is that conversations within the congregation can become accusatory and suspicious as the vulnerability of faith is hardened by the fear of survival as the congregation deals with questions about its present and future identity.

Jesus taught about the need to see beyond self-focused concerns as he extended his second invitation of discipleship in Mark 8:34b-35.

"If any want to become my followers, let them deny themselves and take up their cross and follow me. For those who want to save their life will lose it, and those who lose their life for my sake, and for the sake of the gospel, will save it."

Jesus' first invitation to discipleship had been extended earlier in the Gospel of Mark as he walked by the shore of Galilee and invited Simon, Andrew, James, and John to follow him so they might become fishers of people.

As Jesus passed along the Sea of Galilee, he saw Simon and his brother Andrew casting a net into the sea—for they were fishermen. And Jesus said to them, "Follow me and I will make you fish for people." And immediately they left their nets and followed him. As he went a little farther, he saw James son of Zebedee and his brother John, who were in their boat mending the nets. Immediately he called them; and they left their father Zebedee in the boat with the hired men, and followed him (Mark 1:16-20).

Much had happened between Jesus' initial invitation to discipleship in the first chapter of Mark and his second invitation to discipleship in the eighth chapter of Mark. Signs of vitality abounded as Jesus taught about the reality of God's kingdom. Unclean spirits were cast out, the sick healed, sin forgiven, the dead raised, and the hungry fed. Jesus had calmed a storm and walked on water, but Jesus knew there was a different storm forming as he shared the good news of God's kingdom. As the reality of the cross began to cast its shadow upon Jesus, he issued his second invitation to discipleship by calling his disciples to take up their cross and follow him as they saw beyond self-focused concerns.

In considering Jesus' invitation to discipleship in the first chapter of Mark and the eighth chapter of Mark, it is essential to note that the foundational call of Christian discipleship remained the same. That foundational call is to follow Jesus. It is also essential to note that the context in which Jesus' invitation to follow had changed. The journey of discipleship that had started by the waters of Galilee was now leading to the cross of Calvary.

Christian transformational leaders understand the importance of Jesus' call to follow. It is this call that guides them as they seek to make disciples of Jesus who will transform the world. Understanding the importance of seeing beyond self-focused concerns, they lead movements of hope by following Jesus to the cross of Calvary and the reality of new life that is witnessed through the empty tomb.

For an organization to embrace its present context and the possibility of new realities, it must have the strength to see beyond self-focused concerns as it adapts how it responds to questions about its identity, mission, and purpose. For a congregation to live into the possibility of new realities, it must have the courage to follow Jesus, even when it means that congregation must take up its cross by embracing its present context.

Asking Right Questions: Christian transformational leaders provide guidance for the journey of discipleship by following the third practice of Christian transformational leaders: asking right questions.

Organizational transformation occurs when the goals and behaviors of an organization are aligned with its desired values and future identity. An organization that feels stuck is often one where the conversations within the organization are focused on past or present identity rather than on discerning the desired future identity. When this happens, conversations can be pulled into the direction of self-interest. To change the direction of these conversations, Christian transformational leaders *ask right questions* that allow new conversations to occur. The focus of these questions is designed to allow space for the organization to engage in vulnerable conversations about value and desired identity.

To ask right questions, Christian transformational leaders must first listen to present conversations. Are the conversations about organizational identity based on past realities or a new desired future? Do the conversations invite vulnerability or dictate debate? Do the conversations help discern how to invite people to be followers of Jesus? Are there any signs of organizational transformation that occur as the result of the conversations?

Jesus practiced the art of asking right questions as he listened to the conversations of his disciples:

> They went on from there and passed through Galilee. He did not want anyone to know it; for he was teaching his disciples, saying to them, "The Son of Man is to be betrayed into human hands, and they will kill him, and three days after being killed, he will rise again." But they did not understand what he was saying and were afraid to ask him. Then they came to Capernaum; and when he was in the house he asked them, "What were you arguing about on the way?" But they were silent, for on the way they had argued with one another who was the greatest. He sat down, called

the twelve, and said to them, "Whoever wants to be first must be last of all and servant of all" (Mark 9:30-35).

Consider the context of Jesus' question for his disciples. He had begun to teach them about his upcoming crucifixion and resurrection, but the disciples were not able to comprehend the magnitude of what Jesus was telling them. In their inability to embrace the future journey of discipleship, their conversation turned inward as they argued among themselves about who was the greatest. Jesus responded to their conversation by asking the right question, "What were you arguing about on the way?" Understanding that the intent of right questions is to build community through dialogue, Jesus then sat down with the disciples and taught his recurring message about servanthood.

Today's church finds itself in the grasp of uncertain identity. Change is rapid and certain as congregations discern the best ways to respond faithfully to the mission of making disciples of Jesus Christ for the transformation of the world. The uncertainty of certain change requires congregations to engage in community and build on Jesus' understanding of servant identity if they are going to be relevant in their ministry. Just as the disciples did in Mark 9:30-35, members of congregations can be drawn into a struggle over power and authority when they are uncertain about the future. When this happens, right questions must be asked—questions that change the dialogue from protectionism to mission, from defensiveness to willingness, from the past to the future. This change in the direction of conversations will require congregations to engage in vulnerable conversations that will align their ministry and focus toward a desired identity.

> If a congregation is going to have the mind of Christ, its members must intentionally choose to empty themselves of their own agendas.

Leading by Having the Mind of Christ: Philippians 2:5-11 contains one of the ancient hymns of Christian faith called the "kenosis hymn." "Kenosis" is a Greek word that means self-emptying. The "kenosis hymn" is a song about Jesus' disciples having the mind of Christ among themselves as they follow their Savior in the self-emptying path of Christian servanthood.

Let the same mind be in you that was in Christ Jesus, who, though he was in the form of God, did not regard equality with God as something to be exploited, but emptied himself, taking the form of a slave, being born in human likeness. And being found in human form, he humbled himself and became obedient to the point of death—even death on a cross. Therefore God also highly exalted him and gave him the name that is above every name, so that at the name of Jesus every knee should bend, in heaven and on earth and under the earth, and every tongue should confess that Jesus Christ is Lord, to the glory of God the Father (Philippians 2:5-11).

The words of the "kenosis hymn" witness to the self-emptying love that led Jesus to the cross. It is an invitation for Jesus' followers to understand the nature of Jesus as they seek to follow him in the wisdom of God that appears to be foolishness to the world. As important as the words of the "kenosis hymn" are in understanding the nature of Jesus, they are equally important in understanding the nature of Christ's body. If a congregation is going to have the mind of Christ, its members must intentionally choose to empty themselves of their own agendas as they take on the vision and mission of Jesus Christ. Rather than being driven by the human need to be in control, they are led by the redeemed need to serve. This is when the story of a congregation becomes a song of praise that is in harmony with the story of God's faithfulness. Singing the redeeming song of God's kingdom, the congregation is transformed through the power of Christ's servant nature.

The role of Christian transformational leaders is to live the "kenosis" identity of Jesus as they help congregations define their "kenosis" identity through Jesus. Christian transformational leaders model this identity as they practice the humility of servanthood that led Jesus to empty himself and take the form of a slave. It is this act of self-emptying love that allows the lives of Jesus' followers to become songs of faithfulness to God. It is this self-emptying love that allows a congregation to have the mind of Christ as it follows Jesus in the path of transformational Christian servanthood. Guided by enduring encouragement, a transformed congregation discerns if its ministries are aligned beyond self-focused concerns. Right questions are asked as the whole congregation is invited to engage in conversations about its mission and the context of its ministry. In response, deliberate choices are made as people are invited and equipped to become servant followers of Jesus.

A Case in Point—John's Story

Early in my career, I learned that to excel in business, I had to demonstrate leadership with my peer group. My leadership style was to point out the current reality to my work group, gain their agreement, and then collectively develop a plan to rearrange the status quo and generate a better outcome. I began as a *present-tense leader.* Later in my career, I was responsible for developing long-term strategic plans. My focus was on assessing how to address present and future areas of concern and the opportunities that were available to maximize our company's growth and profitability. I became a *transformational leader.*

When I retired from my business career to enter pastoral ministry, I found that many of my leadership skills transferred to working within the church. The most obvious to me was the congregation's need to have a vision for its future and a strategic plan to reach it. Like the difference between a transformational leader and a Christian transformational leader, however, there is a vast difference between developing a business plan and developing a spiritually based strategic ministry plan.

A congregation's strategic ministry plan is spiritually based and begins with seeking God's leading to discern its mission. Being spiritually based, this plan is naturally focused beyond personal likes and dislikes. Asking the question, "How will this action enable our congregation to be a transformational presence in our community?" becomes the criterion for assessing present and future ministries. It is a holy and daunting endeavor to seek God's leading for a congregation's mission in the world, but remembering God's promises and faithfulness provides the confidence to persevere. Planning a path for the future is a common goal in both plans; however, strategic ministry plans are uniquely developed by listening to God's leading for a congregation, so the congregation can become an effective instrument of transformation in its community.

The importance of listening to God's leading was vividly demonstrated to me in a conversation with a former parishioner. He commented that there were just too many meetings at the church and that the church meetings were just an extension of his day at work. The meetings he led at church and those he led at his place of business were "six of one and half dozen of the other." His statement made an indelible impact on my ministry. It vividly pointed out that the purpose of leadership in the church, whether by laity or clergy, is not simply to conduct business; it is always to listen for God's leading for the purpose of transformation. What I had not fully recognized, or understood, was the need to teach the biblical understanding and imperative of Christian transformational leadership. Sadly, I had not realized that the primary frame of reference for most people to learn leadership skills comes from their secular work experience. It is the church that must teach followers of Jesus how to be servant leaders who can then become transforming forces in their congregations, homes, workplaces, and the world as Christian transformational leaders.

The power and impact of Christian transformational leaders cannot be overemphasized, and it is important to recognize that they can lead from wherever they serve. In a congregation I served, one of my strongest leaders came from a retired family who moved to the area from out of state. I learned that Jan had been a longtime member of The United Methodist Church and had served in various leadership roles. As I got to know her, it was easy to discern her deep and abiding faith, and I looked forward to having her join our leadership team. Unfortunately, when Jan was approached about leading one of the ministries, she declined, saying that she would prefer to be a "worker bee" for a while. Although disappointed at first, I quickly learned that her leadership and influence on our congregation was not dependent on a formal role in the church. It was dependent on her deep and abiding faith, which radiated from her very presence. She embraced Paul's admonition to empty herself and embrace the "mind of Christ" in her daily living. She selflessly served by encouraging others in their faith and offering the wisdom of her faith journey. Although Jan did not initially have a formal role in church leadership, she influenced a countless number of people, many of whom became active in the church's ministries. She was a Christian transformational leader whose purpose was to serve rather than be served. To me, she embodied the essence of Jesus' teaching of servant leadership that is founded in the four practices of a Christian transformational leader: enduring encouragement, seeing beyond self-focused concerns, asking right questions, and leading by having the mind of Christ.

The mission of making disciples of Jesus Christ for the transformation of the world has its foundation in the servanthood of Jesus. To fulfill this mission, the church must align itself with the vision of servanthood that God has revealed through the life, death, and resurrection of Jesus. This alignment requires servants of Christ who are Christian transformational leaders.

——— Questions for Reflection and Discussion ———

1. Why must an organization lose its equilibrium to be transformed? Discuss a time when the chaos of change was manifested in an organization of which you were a part.
2. Consider the ministries of your church. Which ones would be considered inward-focused ministries? outward-focused?
3. Why does organizational transformation occur when the goals and behaviors of an organization are aligned with the values and desired identity of that organization?

CHAPTER TWO

The Ministry of Christian Transformational Leaders

Part One: The Ministry of Christian Transformational Leaders

One of the scribes came near and heard them disputing with one another, and seeing that he answered them well, he asked him, "Which commandment is the first of all?" Jesus answered, "The first is, 'Hear, O Israel: the Lord our God, the Lord is one; you shall love the Lord your God with all your heart, and with all your soul, and with all your mind, and with all your strength.' The second is this, 'You shall love your neighbor as yourself.' There is no other commandment greater than these" (Mark 12:28–31).

The ministry of Christian transformational leaders is manifested by two commandments:

- You shall love the Lord your God with all your heart, and with all your soul, and with all your mind, and with all your strength.
- You shall love your neighbor as yourself.

It is at the intersection of these two commandments that the vision and mission of Jesus' ministry was defined. This intersection of transformation still defines the ministry of Christian transformational leaders as their love for God shapes their present and future identity (vision) and their love for neighbor shapes the relevancy (mission) of their ministry.

John Wesley noted the importance of right relationship as he cited Jesus' two commandments in his sermon titled "On Love."

> The love which our Lord requires in all his followers, is the love of God and man;—of God, for his own, and of man, for God's sake. [1]

An example of the ministry of Christian transformation occurred at a church that encountered skateboarders who were using the parking lot on the church property. The church was beautiful and inviting, but its appeal was not limited to Sunday morning worshipers. The parking lot was ideal for the many skateboarders in the adjacent neighborhoods. The presence of the skateboarders became a point of discussion among church leaders. One young church leader saw an opportunity to be in ministry with the youth of the community. With the blessing of other church leaders, he talked to the skateboarders and the church trustees. These conversations resulted in a surprising turn of events as the church embraced the skateboarders by forming a skateboarding club that included outings to skateboarding sites around the state. "The price" for each trip was the skateboarders listening to a brief reading of Scripture and a prayer. Ultimately, the relationship of the church and skateboarders resulted in a Bible study group. A youth ministry was born. It was through love of God and neighbor that a situation that could have resulted in a message of rejection was transformed into a message of acceptance through the ministry of a Christian transformational leader.

Ephesians describes the foundation for right relationship with God and neighbor. While this epistle was addressed to the "saints in Ephesus," it was a sermon that was circulated among different churches in a time of great transformation, when the identity and mission of Christ's church was established. Ephesians was a favorite biblical book of both John and Charles Wesley because of its emphasis on how the transformative power of God's grace is experienced through Jesus. In his sermon, "Salvation by Faith," based on Ephesians 2:8—"by grace are you saved through faith"—John Wesley states:

> But salvation by faith strikes at the root, and all fall at once where this is established. It was this doctrine, which our Church justly calls the strong rock and foundation of the Christian religion . . .[2]

In this sermon, Wesley witnesses to the saving and transformative power of faith through the life, death, and resurrection of Jesus Christ:

> Christian faith is then, not only an assent to the whole gospel of Christ, but also a full reliance in the blood of Christ; a trust in the merits of his life, death, and resurrection; a recumbency upon him as our atonement and our life, as given for us, and living in us; and in consequence hereof, a closing with him, and cleaving to him, as our "wisdom,

righteousness, sanctification, and redemption," or in one word, our salvation."[3]

In Ephesians, the transformative power of the "whole gospel of Christ" was cited through love of God and neighbor as Jews and Gentiles were reconciled "to God in one body through the cross" (2:16b) and were being "built together spiritually into a dwelling place for God" (2:22b). In Ephesians 3:7, Paul is cited in witnessing how the transformative power of God was experienced in his life as a servant of God's grace: "Of this gospel I have become a servant according to the gift of God's grace that was given me by the working of his power" (3:7).

In his role as a servant of God's grace, Paul practiced the ministry of Christian transformation by leading a movement of hope that defined the early church's identity and ministry. Key to Paul's sermon were the three disciplines of *Christian transformational leadership* that, although addressed to the Ephesians, could be preached in every congregation of the early church as well as every congregation of today's church:

1. Faithful Remembering—connecting with the biblical story of God remembering us
2. Faithful Equipping—aligning with Jesus' call to discipleship
3. Faithful Encouraging—nurturing life in the power of the Holy Spirit.

——— Questions for Reflection and Discussion ———

1. How is the ministry of Christian transformational leaders manifested by Jesus' two commandments?

2. How do Christian transformational leaders respond to the faith and life questions of their day?
3. How is the transformative power of God's grace experienced through Christian servanthood?

Part Two: Faithful Remembering

By *faithfully remembering* the biblical story of God's faithfulness and reclaiming God's vision for the church, Christian transformational leaders are able to faithfully equip and faithfully encourage transformational discipleship.

So then, remember that at one time you Gentiles by birth, called "the uncircumcision" by those who are called "the circumcision"—a physical circumcision made in the flesh by human hands—remember that you were at that time without Christ, being aliens from the commonwealth of Israel, and strangers to the covenants of promise, having no hope and without God in the world. But now in Christ Jesus you who once were far off have been brought near by the blood of Christ. For he is our peace; in his flesh he has made both groups into one and has broken down the dividing wall, that is, the hostility between us. He has abolished the law with its commandments and ordinances, that he might create in himself one new humanity in place of the two, thus making peace, and might reconcile both groups to God in one body through the cross, thus putting to death that hostility through it. So he came and proclaimed peace to you who were far off and peace to those who were near for through him both of us have access in one Spirit to the Father. So then you are no longer strangers and aliens, but you are citizens with the saints and also members of the household of God, built upon the foundation of the apostles and prophets, with Christ Jesus himself as the cornerstone. In him the whole structure is joined together and grows into a holy temple in the Lord; in whom you also are built together spiritually into a dwelling place for God (Ephesians 2:11-22).

The epistle to Ephesians is an invitation to faithfully remember how God reconciles Jesus' followers into one faithful body by "breaking down the dividing wall through Jesus." The church in Ephesus, as are all churches, was founded on the principle that *faithful remembering* is required for both formation and transformation. A key component of *faithful remembering* is that God remembers us for who God created us to be. God also remembers us for who God loves and expects us to be as individuals, leaders, and as communities of faith. Remembering that they are "built together spiritually into a dwelling place for God," all followers of Jesus are called to be part of the story of God's redemption as they "are citizens with the saints and also members of the household of God." The goal of faithful remembering is to provide the foundation for Christian transformation that is aligned with God's will.

The goal of *faithful remembering* is to provide the foundation for Christian transformation that is aligned with God's will.

Rather than being an activity of the past tense, faithful remembering focuses on the future tense of faith as in Christ, "the whole structure is joined together and grows into a holy temple in the Lord." It is the future tense of faithful remembering that shapes the vision and identity of Christian transformational leaders and establishes the foundation of their ministry.

An example of faithful remembering occurs in Mary's Magnificat in Luke 1:46-55. Mary, the expectant mother of Jesus, is greeted with a blessing by her cousin Elizabeth, who is the expectant mother of John the Baptist. In response, Mary sings the story of God's faithfulness:

> My soul magnifies the Lord, and my spirit rejoices in God my Savior, for he has looked with favor on the lowliness of his servant. Surely, from now on all generations will call me blessed: for the Mighty One has done great things for me, and holy is his name. His mercy is for those who fear him from generation to generation. He has shown strength with his arm; he has scattered the proud in the thoughts of their hearts. He has brought down the powerful from their thrones, and lifted up the lowly; he has filled the hungry with good things, and sent the rich away empty. He has helped his servant Israel, in remembrance of his mercy, according to the promise he made to our ancestors, to Abraham and to his descendants forever.

The theme of Mary's Magnificat is God's continual mercy on "those who fear him from generation to generation." It was in the act of remembering God's faithfulness that Mary sang her song of faith as she remembered God's mercy that extends from one generation to the next. It is faithful remembering that will sustain Mary as she gives birth to Jesus and a new understanding of how future generations will trust in God's faithfulness through the life of the Savior who was entrusted to her care. Faithfully remembering God's steadfast mercy, Mary sang the song of God's faithfulness as she encountered God in the presence of her unborn son, Jesus.

Christian transformational leaders sing the song of God's faithfulness as they encounter God through the presence of Jesus. Faithfully remembering that the Bible tells the story of the faithful creating and redeeming God, their leadership is undergirded in God's continual mercy. Answering God's call upon their lives in the present, they live into the future promise of God's faithfulness as their souls magnify the Lord and their spirits rejoice in God their Savior whose mercy is promised from one generation to the next.

They understand the purpose of faithful remembering that is found in Paul's advice to Timothy in I Timothy 6:17-19 as the apostle encourages the young leader to hold fast to the richness of faith that is found in God's faithfulness:

> As for those who in the present age are rich, command them not to be haughty, or to set their hopes on the uncertainty of riches, but rather on God who richly provides us with everything for our enjoyment. They are to do good, to be rich in good works, generous, and ready to share, thus storing up for themselves the treasure of a good foundation for the future, so that they may take hold of the life that really is life (I Timothy 6:17-19).

Following Paul's advice to Timothy, Christian transformational leaders store "up for themselves the treasure of a good foundation for the future, so that they may take hold of the life that really is life." The direction of their ministry is aligned with trust in God "who richly provides everything." While transformational leaders shape the future by basing their visions and strategies on organizational goals, Christian transformational leaders shape the future by faithfully remembering the biblical story of God's faithfulness as they lead congregations to and through faithful discussions that facilitate an alignment of congregational life with the biblical story of God's faithfulness.

A Case in Point—John's Story

One of my appointments began with a significant challenge. For a variety of reasons, I started my appointment with the church offerings in significant decline. During the next year, the offerings dropped about one third—a significant decline for any size church. The council's emotions were high from the resulting anxiety they felt with such a precipitous decline. The first challenge was how to reduce the anxiety in the council and to help them look toward the future and not be overwhelmed by the present dilemma. In other words, given the current reality, how could the church move forward with a faithful response toward a brighter future? I knew developing a budget plan to stabilize the finances was critical for the immediate future, but I also recognized the long-term need to engender hope and remind the congregation that its call to mission in the world had not changed. The nature and type of its ministries might be different, but the holy purpose of its origin did not change. It was critical that the church council members understand that regardless of current financial restraints, the need to align the congregation's life with the biblical story of faith remained.

A savvy executive who had taken early retirement agreed to lead this initiative. Beverly had a deep and abiding faith and was a lifelong member of the church. Her family had been active participants in the church's leadership for more than fifty years. This history with the church enabled her to give a living testimony to God's faithfulness in the past. She was able to use her history and her passion for the church to provide the leadership needed to move from the present concerns toward a faithful future she knew God would reveal. She reminded the members of the congregation that the current reality need not get in the way of their mission. She encouraged them to remember God's past faithfulness with their church as seen in the biblical record of God's presence and power in the world. She reminded them that there had been many challenges in the church's 200-plus-year history, but that God's faithfulness and empowering presence had enabled previous generations of this congregation to look forward in spite of challenges. She pointed out that her parents' generation chose to build a new sanctuary in anticipation of future generations. They were standing on the shoulders of all the followers of Jesus who had come before. This faithful remembering of God's ever-present faithfulness and love enabled them to focus beyond the present and look toward the future with hope and confidence.

It was only a few years later that this congregation would embark on a significant building project. They chose to faithfully remember God's faithfulness and to keep aligned with the church's mission to make disciples of Jesus Christ for the transformation of the world.

—— **Questions for Reflection and Discussion** ——

1. Why is it important for Christian transformational leaders to first faithfully remember?
2. As a church leader, how are you practicing the discipline of faithful remembering?
3. Can you identify areas of your congregation's mission that reflect faithful remembering?

Part Three: Faithful Equipping

But each of us was given grace according to the measure of Christ's gift. Therefore it is said, "When he ascended on high he made captivity itself a captive; he gave gifts to his people." . . . The gifts he gave were that some would be apostles, some prophets, some evangelists, some pastors and teachers, to equip the saints for the work of ministry, for building up the body of Christ, until all of us come to the unity of the faith and of the knowledge of the Son of God, to maturity, to the measure of the full stature of Christ. We must no longer be children, tossed to and fro and blown about by every wind of doctrine, by people's trickery, by their craftiness in deceitful scheming. But speaking the truth in love, we must grow up in every way into him who is the head, into Christ, from whom the whole body, joined and knit together by every ligament with which it is equipped, as each part is working properly, promotes the body's growth in building itself up in love (Ephesians 4:7-8, 11-16).

The goal of faithful equipping is to help people align their lives with Jesus' call to discipleship. The desired outcome of faithful equipping is a community of faithful disciples who will seek to answer God's call upon their lives and the life of their congregation. Their faith in Jesus will shape their mission as they seek to be disciples and make disciples of Jesus Christ for the transformation of the world. This movement of transformation will occur as communities of Jesus' followers connect their stories of faith to the story of God's faithfulness. Christian transformational leaders accomplish this goal as they faithfully equip church members and leaders to follow the biblical directives in Ephesians 4:15-16:

- Speak the truth in love
- Grow up in every way into him who is the head, into Christ
- Help the whole body to be joined and knit together by every ligament with which it is equipped, as each part is working properly
- Promote the body's growth in building itself up in love.

A Case in Point—John Wesley's Story
John Wesley emphasized the biblical directives of Ephesians 4:15-16 as he equipped people within the Methodist

movement through the formation of circles where they covenanted to speak the truth in love as they grew together in Christian faith. Seeking to equip followers of Jesus as they sought to align their lives with the biblical story of faith, Wesley emphasized the "means of grace." Identifying the Methodist movement through his emphasis on "personal holiness" and "social holiness," he taught about two disciplines through which God's grace is experienced in the lives of followers of Jesus: works of piety (love of God) and works of mercy (love of neighbor).

Upon these foundations, Wesley established the identity and mission of Methodism. The identity and mission that Wesley established still has the power to transform the lives of Jesus' disciples in today's church.

Works of piety are individual and communal disciplines of spiritual formation that shape the life and faith of a follower of Jesus. For Wesley, these individual disciplines included (among others) prayer, study of the Scriptures, fasting, regular attendance of worship, sharing of faith, and healthy living. Wesley also emphasized the importance of gathering with fellow Christians through communal disciplines such as the sharing of sacraments, Bible study, and faithful accountability.

Works of mercy are individual and communal acts of discipleship that witness to God's grace and justice. Wesley taught that individual disciplines of mercy included feeding the hungry, visiting the sick, doing good works, visiting those in prison, and giving generously to those in need. Communal disciplines of mercy included advocacy for justice, ending oppression, and responding to the needs of the poor.

When the identity of a congregation is defined by the means of grace, transformation occurs in the life of the individual and in the life of the faith community. The ministry of the congregation becomes a manifestation of the work of the Holy Spirit, and vitality becomes a reality that is defined as the Greatest Commandment is realized in individual and communal acts of discipleship. As this happens, the identity of a vital congregation is defined by Paul's vision of the church as found in Philippians 2:1-4:

> If then there is any encouragement in Christ, any consolation from love, any sharing in the Spirit, any compassion and sympathy, make my joy complete: be of the same mind, having the same love, being in full accord and of one mind. Do nothing from selfish ambition or conceit, but in humility regard others as better than yourselves. Let each of you look not to your own interests, but to the interests of others.

It is this vision of vitality that Christian transformational leaders remember as they equip individuals and congregations to fulfill the mission of making disciples of Jesus Christ for the transformation of the world. It is not an easy path to follow, as the cost of discipleship requires love of God and love of neighbor. It is, however, the only path to follow if the Great Commandment is to be realized in the life of Jesus' followers. Christian transformational leaders help to equip others to follow the Great Commandment by first living in the means of grace and then leading others to practice the means of grace in their own lives. *The Book of Discipline* outlines how lay servants may assist in leading a congregation in fulfilling the discipline of faithful equipping. This disciplinary role of servant leadership will be discussed more fully in the next chapter.

—— **Questions for Reflection and Discussion** ——

1. In what ways does your leadership reflect a commitment to faithful equipping?
2. How is your leadership connected and aligned with the Great Commandment of loving God and neighbor?
3. How have the means of grace influenced your faith journey?

Part Four: Faithful Encouraging

Knowing that, at times, it is easier to walk away from discipleship in Jesus than to walk in discipleship with Jesus, Christian transformational leaders faithfully encourage life that is empowered by the Holy Spirit. Jesus taught his disciples about life that is empowered by the Holy Spirit in the Gospel of John as he prepared his disciples to walk in discipleship after his impending crucifixion and resurrection:

And I will ask the Father, and he will give you another Advocate, to be with you forever. This is the Spirit of truth, whom the world cannot receive, because it neither sees him nor knows him. You know him, because he abides with you, and he will be in you (John 14:16-17).

But the Advocate, the Holy Spirit, whom the Father will send in my name, will teach you everything, and remind you of all that I have said to you (John 14:26).

The last two chapters of Ephesians contain words of faithful encouragement for a Spirit-empowered life of discipleship:

Be filled with the Spirit, as you sing psalms and hymns and spiritual songs among yourselves, singing and making melody to the Lord in your hearts, giving thanks to God the Father at all times and for everything in the name of our Lord Jesus Christ (Ephesians 5:18b-20).

Pray in the Spirit at all times in every prayer and supplication. To that end keep alert and always persevere in supplication for all the saints (Ephesians 6:18).

Biblical teachings about God's Spirit are not confined to the New Testament. The Old Testament contains numerous references to God's Spirit that shape the Christian understanding of the Holy Spirit. The Book of Isaiah speaks of the servant of God who will be faithful to God's calling because of the presence of God's Spirit:

The spirit of the Lord God is upon me, because the Lord has anointed me; he has sent me to bring good news to the oppressed, to bind up the brokenhearted, to proclaim liberty to the captives, and release to the prisoners; to proclaim the year of the Lord's favor (Isaiah 61:1-2a).

Jesus would claim these prophetic words about the power of God's Spirit as he announced the beginning of his ministry.

When he came to Nazareth, where he had been brought up, he went to the synagogue on the sabbath day, as was his custom. He stood up to read, and the scroll of the prophet Isaiah was given to him. He unrolled the scroll and found the place where it was written; "The Spirit of the Lord is upon me, because he has anointed me to bring good news to the poor. He has sent me to proclaim release to the captives and recovery of sight to the blind, to proclaim the year of the Lord's favor." And he rolled up the scroll, gave it back to the attendant, and sat down. The eyes of all in the synagogue were fixed on him. Then he began to say to them, "Today this scripture has been fulfilled in your hearing" (Luke 4:16-21).

The Book of Joel contains words of encouragement about how the Spirit of God will strengthen the lives of God's people:

Then afterward I will pour out my spirit on all flesh, your sons and your daughters shall prophesy, your old men shall dream dreams, and your young men shall see visions. Even on the male and female slaves, in those days, I will pour out my spirit (Joel 2:28-29).

Peter would claim these prophetic words as he announced the birth of the church on the day of Pentecost.

No, this is what was spoken through the prophet Joel: 'In the last days it will be, God declares, that I will pour my

Spirit upon all flesh, and your sons and your daughters will prophesy, and your young men shall see visions, and your old men shall dream dreams. Even upon my slaves, both men and women, in those days I will pour out my Spirit' (Acts 2:16-18).

Throughout the Bible, the consistent message of faith is that life is lived fully when life is empowered by God. The creation account found in the second chapter of Genesis tells of God breathing the fullness of life into the first human:

Then the Lord God formed man from the dust of the ground, and breathed into his nostrils the breath of life; and the man became a living being (Genesis 2:7).

The resurrection account of Jesus that is found in John 20:19-23 affirms the understanding of God breathing God's fullness of life into Jesus' disciples:

When it was evening on that day, the first day of the week, and the doors of the house where the disciples had met were locked for fear of the Jews, Jesus came and stood among them and said, "Peace be with you." After he said this, he showed them his hands and his side. Then the disciples rejoiced when they saw the Lord. Jesus said to them again, "Peace be with you. As the Father has sent me, so I send you." When he had said this, he breathed on them and said to them, "Receive the Holy Spirit. If you forgive the sins of any, they are forgiven them; if you retain the sins of any, they are retained."

Followers of Jesus believe the Holy Spirit empowers fullness of life through Jesus. It is this encouraging message that offers hope to their lives as they encounter the reality of the crucified and risen Christ. In turn, they share the encouraging message of the crucified and risen Christ as they witness to the fullness of God's presence. It is the ministry of a Christian transformational leader to faithfully encourage people to live with enduring faith in Jesus. Hebrews 12:1-3 is an example of how the author of Hebrews practiced the ministry of faithful encouraging:

> Therefore, since we are surrounded by so great a cloud of witnesses, let us also lay aside every weight and the sin that clings so closely, and let us run with perseverance the race that is set before us, looking to Jesus the pioneer and perfecter of our faith, who for the sake of the joy that was set before him endured the cross, disregarding its shame, and has taken his seat at the right hand of the throne of God. Consider him who endured such hostility against himself from sinners, so that you may not grow weary or lose heart.

Some within the congregation of the Hebrews were beginning to wander from the faith of Jesus. In turn, many were in danger of losing hope. The congregation of the Hebrews was standing at a critical moment. Within the reality of this context, the Letter to the Hebrews was written to faithfully encourage these followers of Jesus to keep the focus of their ministry on Jesus as they encountered challenges to their faith and their lives. Within the current context of the church, there are many congregations that identify with the congregation of the Hebrews. Vitality seems

> The goal of *faithful encouraging* is to help followers of Jesus keep the focus of their ministry on Jesus.

to be a distant dream. Questions about the future cloud the vision of the present. It is within this current context that the Christian transformational discipline of faithful encouraging is essential for the present and future ministry of Jesus' followers.

A Case in Point—Marc's Story

I arrived as pastor of my first church on a Thursday. There were no advance meetings between appointed pastors and church leadership in those days, so the first time I met anyone from the church in person was on moving day. Three days later I worshiped with my new church family for the first time. I carefully prepared a seven-page single-spaced sermon that would help to inspire confidence in my spiritual leadership of this congregation. In preparing to lead worship, I asked the lay leader where I should wait for the service of worship to begin. He told me I should go to the small room on the front right side of the sanctuary. I asked the lay leader how I would know to begin the service of worship and was informed an acolyte would join me in that room. When the acolyte went out of the room to light the candles, worship would begin.

At 10:45, I went into the little room on the front right side of the sanctuary. At 10:50, the organist began playing "Little Church in the Wildwood," and the acolyte came into the little room where I was seated. We talked about his family and his school. At 11:00, I looked at my watch and thought it was time for worship to begin, but I knew the instructions I had received—worship would begin when the acolyte went out of the room to light the candles. At 11:05, the acolyte and I were still talking and the organist was still playing "Little Church in the Wildwood" when the lay leader opened the door to the room and asked if everything was all right. I assured the lay leader that all was fine and that the acolyte and I were having a good conversation. At about 11:08, I asked the acolyte if the service of worship should be starting soon. He said, "We wait for the choir to go out before we go out." I said, "The choir's not singing today." He put his hand to his forehead and said, "Oh, I forgot."

At 11:10, I followed the acolyte out of the small room into the sanctuary. The organist, who had been playing "Little Church in the Wildwood" non-stop for twenty minutes, gave me a look that let me know worship was late in beginning. I sat down while the acolyte was lighting the candles and thought I had to say something that would let the congregation know the wisdom of the bishop in appointing me to be the pastor of their church community. When the candles had been lit and the organist had stopped playing, I stood up before the congregation, smiled, and said, "Good things are worth waiting for."

Nobody laughed. I was so nervous that, by the grace of God, my seven-page single-spaced sermon took five minutes to preach, and the service concluded before noon.

At the reception following worship, instead of focusing on my late start of the worship service, the members of that church transformed what could have been a devastating experience through extravagant grace-filled encouragement as they told me how glad they were the bishop had appointed me to be the pastor of their church. Through their *faithful encouraging*, I experienced the powerful hope of the Holy Spirit and the fullness of God's grace. The next Sunday, worship began at 11:00.

—— Questions for Reflection and Discussion ——

1. How does your leadership demonstrate faithful encouraging?
2. What are some specific ways you can expand your efforts to be a faithful encourager?
3. Why is the Holy Spirit necessary for Christian transformation?

Part Five: John Wesley

As the church encounters new understandings of God's faithfulness, it is good to remember how John Wesley practiced the disciplines of *faithful remembering*, *faithful equipping*, and *faithful encouraging*.

The challenges the church is encountering in today's world are reflected in the challenges the church encountered in the world of Wesley's time. Questions of identity and relevancy plagued the church as it separated itself from responding to pressing societal needs such as poverty, slavery, lack of education, and corruption that were present throughout England. It was in the reality of these needs and this time of questioning that the Methodist movement began as John Wesley employed the three disciplines of Christian transformational leadership.

The foundation of faithful remembering was laid early in John Wesley's life when a fire destroyed the rectory in which his family lived. As the family escaped the fire, it was discovered that John (at that time, six years of age) was still inside the home. John was seen standing at a window; then a neighbor lifted a man to his shoulders and removed John from the burning house moments before the roof caved in. Wesley would often identify himself as a "brand snatched from the burning" as he recalled this incident and sensed God's call upon his life. One of the people who was instrumental in laying the foundation of faithful remembering in John Wesley's life was his mother, Susanna. The mother of nineteen children (ten of whom lived to maturity), Susanna spent individual time with each child with the goal of developing strong principles of Christian faith.

Another instrumental foundation of faithful remembering occurred early in John Wesley's ministry when he joined the "Holy Club" that his brother Charles had begun at Oxford. It was within this incubator of discipleship that participants vowed to lead holy lives as they faithfully remembered God's claim upon their lives by receiving the Eucharist weekly, praying and studying the Bible daily, visiting the ill and people in prison. This foundation of discipleship would shape Wesley as he formed the structure of the Methodist movement that would provide accountability for people who desired to be followers of Jesus.

As a priest in the Church of England, Wesley would not let go of a desire for personal and social holiness as he faithfully remembered the mission of being a disciple of Jesus Christ and the reality of the church of his day. Even though he encountered times of personal questioning regarding his own faith and disappointing results with his ministry, Wesley persistently held fast to his desire for being a follower of Jesus. The outcome of this desire for discipleship was manifested on May 24, 1738, on Aldersgate Street. Wesley recounts this experience in his journal:

> In the evening, I went very unwillingly to a society in Aldersgate-Street, where one was reading Luther's preface to the Epistle to the Romans. About a quarter before nine, while he was describing the change which God works in the heart through faith in Christ, I felt my heart strangely warmed. I felt I did trust in Christ, Christ alone for salvation, and an assurance was given *me* that he had taken away *my* sins, even *mine*, and saved *me* from the law of sin and death.[4]

It was this heartwarming experience that would undergird Wesley as he equipped people to become disciples of Jesus through the structuring of the Methodist movement. Through the formation of societies, bands, class meetings, the General Rules of the societies, preaching houses, *The Sunday Service of the Methodists*, and *The Articles of Religion*, Wesley established ways for people to express and live Christian discipleship. The goal of the discipleship groupings of societies, classes, and bands was the creation of a culture of relationship and accountability through prayer, study, confession, and encouragement. Each group was designed to lead participants to deeper faith in Jesus as they watched over one another in love. Group members were challenged and equipped to live their faith with deeper accountability as they responded to various guiding questions. For United Societies, the guiding question was "do you desire to flee from the wrath to come, to be saved of your sins?" Classes, formed out of the societies based on geographical location of class members, had a guiding question of "how does your soul prosper?" Bands, formed out of Wesley's interaction with the Moravians, were based on the desire for the deepest level of relationship and accountability, as admission to a band required a member to answer questions such as, "Do you desire to be told of all your faults . . . ?"

Wesley was an active participant in the process of developing Christian disciples as he faithfully equipped and faithfully encouraged the Wesleyan movement. He traveled over 250,000 miles, preaching over 40,000 sermons, teaching, and exhorting faithfulness in Christ. His sermons and writings were published along with his explanatory notes on the Bible. Practicing both personal and social holiness, he became an advocate for the poor through his personal charity, the establishment of schools, and the establishment of medical dispensaries. He also addressed larger societal issues as a persistent advocate for the abolition of slavery.

Throughout the whole experience of the Wesleyan Movement, John Wesley practiced the three disciplines of Christian transformational leadership as he faithfully remembered, faithfully equipped, and faithfully encouraged people to profess and live faith in Jesus Christ. It is through the practice of these disciplines that lay servants become Christian transformational leaders as they live the mission of making disciples of Jesus Christ for the transformation of the world.

The disciplines of *Christian transformational leadership* are not limited to life in a congregation.

The disciplines of Christian transformational leadership are not limited to life in a congregation. They can result in transformation in any setting.

A Case in Point—Kathy's Story

As the top-ranking operations executive for a large company, I had a huge amount of positional power and authority—company planes, corner offices, support staff, reserved parking spots, and so on. My challenge as a Christian transformational leader was to not let these perks define me as a person or as a leader. I had to discern how to serve this large organization while leading it. I was a student of secular theories of effective leadership for many years. As I began exploring biblical teachings about leadership, I was astonished and humbled to learn that all of the theories I had studied were rooted in Scripture.

The first notion that rang so true for me was that every single person in the organization offered the same level of potential and value. We might have different jobs to do, but no job made anyone more important as a human than another. Isn't that the beginning point for one of the greatest commandments to "Love your neighbor as yourself"? An executive who believes this naturally seeks processes and structures that require excellence while still being fair and valuing people.

The next notion that was clear in both biblical and secular teaching on effective leadership was one of servant leadership. As an executive, I believed that the people of the organization could and would deliver the right outcomes in the right way if they had what they needed to do so. They needed interesting work that came with clarity about how to be successful. They needed the information, technology, and tools to be efficient and effective. They needed reward systems that recognized their hard work and their successes. They needed opportunities for a work–life balance. They needed supervisors who valued them and loved them enough to tell them the truth about their performance—sharing the recognition when they were excelling and supporting them if their performance was falling short. The authority that my position carried allowed me to require and sometimes design these approaches (policies, processes, rules, incentives, pay scales, training curricula, hiring procedures, performance management processes, etc.). But often, the "way we've always done it" was a stumbling block to progress.

It was hard to stay in this humble yet powerful position. The power kept trying to take over and define me. When I declined a corner office with windows so that the rest of the employees could have access to the light and the view, it was norm-shattering. As you can imagine, many people who craved those signs of power did not like my decision one bit. When I established a practice that empty seats on the company plane could be booked by any employee who was traveling to the same destination, there was much resistance. The 'policy' didn't allow this. These examples show how the hierarchy was ingrained in the fabric of the organization and maintained the status quo.

It is possible for executives in the secular world as well as church leaders to lead as Christian transformational leaders. It requires the ability to see what real success for the future (not the past) looks like. It requires organizational savvy as the vision is articulated and the organization is aligned to deliver on that vision. And it requires a true servant leader heart as one leads with the authority that springs from Jesus' teachings of loving God and neighbor as ourselves.

For the mission of the church to be fulfilled as disciples are made of Jesus Christ for the transformation of the world, Christian transformational leaders must practice the disciplines of Christian transformation in both their communities of faith and in their places of interaction with the world. This mission will become reality as disciples of Jesus live in relationship with the risen Christ through their community of faith and are sent out into the world to proclaim the message of right relationship with their neighbors. Realizing any change that is void of ongoing relationship with God and neighbor will result in only a temporary response to the present questions of faith and life, they practice the Christian transformational disciplines of *faithful remembering*, *faithful equipping*, and *faithful encouraging*. Servants of grace rather than masters of change, they lead movements of hope as they respond to the life and faith questions of their day by loving the Lord their God with all their heart, soul, mind, and strength, and by loving their neighbor as themselves. This is the ministry of Christian transformational leaders.

——— Questions for Reflection and Discussion ———

1. In what ways was John Wesley a Christian transformational leader?
2. How can you be a Christian transformational leader in settings other than your church?
3. Love for God shapes the present and future identity (vision), and love for neighbor shapes the relevancy (mission) of a congregation's ministry. How might these teachings of Jesus be taught and implemented in your congregation?

CHAPTER THREE

Defining Congregational Vitality

Part One: Defining Congregational Vitality

What is the impetus for The United Methodist Church's emphasis on congregational vitality? What constitutes a vital congregation? Why does a vital congregation matter? To answer these questions, we travel to the 2008 General Conference when the mission statement of The United Methodist Church was expanded from "The mission of the Church is to make disciples of Jesus Christ" to "The mission of the Church is to make disciples of Jesus Christ for the transformation of the world."[1] With the addition of *"for the transformation of the world,"* The United Methodist Church's mission became focused with the expectation that the evidence of Christian discipleship is transformation. It is important to note that while the expectation of transformation was added to the mission statement, the understanding of where disciples of Jesus Christ are made continued to focus on the local church, as the second sentence of the mission statement remained the same:

Local churches provide the most significant arena through which disciple-making occurs.[2]

"The mission of the Church is to make disciples of Jesus Christ *for the transformation of the world.*"

In response to the expanded mission statement and the missional expectation that a local church provides fertile soil for both Christian discipleship and the transformation of the world, a Call to Action Project was begun by The Council of Bishops (composed of all the bishops of The United Methodist Church) and the Connectional Table (the general church body that is responsible for oversight of the vision of The United Methodist Church). In January 2010, The Call to Action Steering Team was begun and assigned with the task of assessing and aligning denominational resources with the mission statement that was approved by the 2008 General Conference. A foundational part of The Call to Action Steering Team's work included data from more than 32,000 United Methodist congregations, which were the subjects of a rigorous research and analysis effort. The report concluded that high-vitality churches consistently share common factors that work together to influence congregational vitality and are characterized by the prevalence of:

- effective pastoral leadership, including inspirational preaching, mentoring laity, and effective management
- multiple small groups and programs for children and youth
- a mix of traditional and contemporary worship services

- a high percentage of spiritually engaged laity who assume leadership roles.[3]

In response to the report by the Call to Action Steering Team, a denominational reporting tool "VitalSigns" (www.umc.org/how -we-serve/vitalsign-dashboard) was launched in January 2011. The VitalSigns dashboard includes the following measurements: average weekly attendance, professions of faith, small groups, members in mission, and dollars given to mission.

For a minimum of ten years, beginning January 2011, congregations are expected to report and assess signs of vitality in the areas of worship attendance, professions of faith, small groups, engagement in mission, and giving to mission. To assist in assessing VitalSigns data, United Methodist congregations were encouraged to establish 2013-2016 quadrennial goals that, in turn, were presented by the Council of Bishops during an act of worship at the 2012 General Conference. The expectation was that VitalSigns data would allow congregations to continually assess their progress toward vitality. Response to VitalSigns has been mixed. Some annual conferences have embraced it. Some incorporated it into other reporting instruments. Some chose not to participate.

There are two primary ways that organizations respond to data. The first is a natural, but regrettable, response as people fear the consequences of a new measurement system. Their conversations are focused on "the numbers" rather than on vision and mission. This response rarely leads to congregational vitality. Alternatively, vital congregations allow data to drive creative conversations that inspire new behaviors. These new behaviors, in turn, result in new outcomes that lead to congregational vitality and are ultimately *reflected* in "the numbers."

Regardless of a congregation's starting point, forward movement requires new and creative conversations in these critical areas:

- Vital Vision and Mission
- Vital Leadership
- Vital Discipleship
- Vital Alignment

—— Questions for Reflection and Discussion ——

1. What are conversations like in a church that uses numbers rather than mission as its driving force?
2. What are examples of the characteristics of a vital congregation that is guided by mission?
3. How can a local church provide fertile soil for both Christian discipleship and the transformation of the world?

Part Two: Vital Vision and Mission

Vital congregations are focused on WHY (vision) they exist and WHAT (mission) they are called to do because of why they exist.

All who believed were together and had all things in common; they would sell their possessions and goods and distribute the proceeds to all, as any had need. Day by day, as they spent much time together in the temple, they broke bread at home and ate their food with glad and generous hearts, praising God and having the goodwill of all the people. And day by day the Lord added to their number those who were being saved (Acts 2:44-47).

Luke's account of the early church provides a portrait of vital vision and mission through the use of the word "all." Recognizing that Christian discipleship is a communal act of faith, the key descriptors that Luke used to describe the vision and mission of the early church are:

- *All* who believed were together.
- Had *all* things in common.
- Sold their possessions and goods and distributed the proceeds to *all*, as any had need.
- Praised God and had the good will of *all* the people.

John Wesley embraced the early church's example of communal faith by teaching the disciplines of works of piety (love of God) and works of mercy (love of neighbor) as a way for *all* of life to be lived. Disciples were to be actively engaged in faith that encompassed both disciplines. Many churches forget the fundamental need to identify their purpose based on both love of God and love of neighbor. They either focus on becoming an attractional church that emphasizes programming and worship or becoming a missional church that emphasizes works of charity. Christ's vision and mission for his followers is to be witnesses of new life where both love of God and love of neighbor defines the way of discipleship. To be faithful to their purpose, churches must be both attractional (offering relevant programming and worship) and missional (building transformational relationships with people in their community rather than simply engaging in acts of charity). This collective missional and attractional focus empowers a congregation to be a sanctuary of Christian transformation.

As discussed in the previous chapter, the vision of Jesus' followers is to love God with all their heart, mind, soul, and strength. Guided by their love for God, they live with the mission of loving their neighbors as themselves. Vital congregations allow these two commandments to shape their present and future vision and mission. Focused by the two great commandments of Jesus, they assess the vitality of their congregations through the foundation of spiritual formation and acts of justice. Grounded in the acts of piety and acts of mercy that formed the Wesleyan movement, they look for signs of transformation within their congregation and within their community. Through the context of love of God and love of neighbor, the goal for their ministry is for people within their congregation to live in redeeming relationship with one another and for their congregation to live in redeeming relationship with their local and global community. When this goal is realized, transformation occurs. When this goal is not realized, the vision and mission of a congregation will fade as a congregation deals with a declining influence in its community and the inevitable declining numbers in its congregation.

One of the reasons this focus fades is because the mission is not well-defined, inspiring, or actionable. Sometimes congregations struggle with discerning their mission and what they perceive to be the daunting task of developing a mission statement. In its most simple form, the following question makes this sacred task possible: "Why has God put these people with these hearts, skills, and resources in this place at this time?"

Christian transformational leaders can help their congregation discern their own statement of mission. Many books and consultants offer detailed processes for discerning an organization's mission. A basic but comprehensive process for the development of a congregation's mission has the following steps.

1. Enter a time of prayerful discernment.
2. Determine who your surrounding neighbors are (define your community).
3. Gather facts and learn about your neighbors (environmental analysis).
4. Determine what you, as a congregation, do really well (core competencies).
5. Discuss how your Christian influence should impact your community and the world (changed condition).
6. Pull those thoughts together in one or two sentences (statement of mission).
7. Establish ways the mission can be accomplished (set goals).

When a congregation enters into a time of prayerful discernment and follows this simple process, the results are sure to be grounded in love of God and love of neighbor.

Vital congregations are focused on WHY (vision) they exist and WHAT (mission) they are called to do because of why they exist.

A Case in Point—Kathy's Story

United Methodist congregations are called to "make disciples of Jesus Christ for the transformation of the world." This is the story of a medium-sized congregation that struggled with how to do that in a community that was changing rapidly. The church was experiencing declining membership involvement and subsequent membership decline. The community around the church was changing rapidly, and church members found they had less and less in common with the new community residents.

The church tried a new worship style, a refocus on the youth ministry, many fellowship opportunities, and so on. They were clear about what they were trying to do—get people to come to church so they could tell them the good news of Jesus Christ. But no matter what they tried, the people weren't coming. The leaders of the church decided to take some time in prayerful discernment. They were clear that their vision (WHY they exist) was "to make disciples of Jesus Christ for the transformation of the world." But they realized that they were unclear about their mission (WHAT they are called to do because of why they exist). As they began to ponder and pray about this, they began to discuss the gifts, skills, and resources God had given them. They began to ask, "What are we really good at?" and "Why did God put us in this place, at this time, with these gifts?"

Their community was rapidly changing, as a huge apartment complex was being built about two miles from the church. A largely minority population was moving into the apartment complex, and the members of the church had no idea how best to communicate with the new members of the community. Initially the church resisted the construction of the apartments because church members feared the community would change too much and begin to decline. But the apartments were built, the resident population was forming, and the church felt called to reach out to the people.

As the church discussed what they were really good at, they mentioned several times how they "kicked into high gear when a baby was born" in their congregation. They cooked and made useful baby items for the family. Current parents and grandparents visited the families regularly to offer food, care items, babysitting, comfort, and advice. The realization that "we are good when a baby is born" led a few key leaders to ask the question, "How can we put these skills to work for the new members of our community?" "How can we reach out to our neighbors to love them as ourselves?" Some members were excited about these new opportunities, while others were uncomfortable or resistant. But a small group of members moved forward to design and organize an approach for "loving on the new babies and families of our community." They extended their successful ministry to families of newborns in the apartment complex. Flyers detailing the ministry were distributed. The connection started slowly, but it grew over time. Church members brought a home-cooked meal, a hand-knitted baby blanket, encouragement, and offers of help to the families of newborns. Relationships were formed at this wonderful, scary, overwhelming time in a family's life. As these relationships grew, the church was able to find other ways to reach out and love their neighbors as themselves. Over time, the ministries of the church began to change, and members of the community began to come. It is a long, prayerful, intentional process that continues today, and it all began with the question of "Why did God put us in this place at this time with these gifts?" And as they decided to "love on the babies and families of this community," they backed into this statement of their mission: "This church is here to love our neighbors as ourselves and to share the good news of Jesus Christ as we grow in faith together."

——— Questions for Reflection and Discussion ———

1. What are some things that your church does really well? Discuss ways your church can adapt these gifts to serve your local community.
2. Why is it important to emphasize both love of God and love of neighbor? What is the danger of neglecting one or the other?
3. How are Wesley's emphases on works of piety and works of mercy realized in today's congregations?

Part Three: Vital Leadership

Paul, Silvanus, and Timothy,
To the church of the Thessalonians in God the Father and the Lord Jesus Christ: Grace to you and peace. We always

give thanks to God for all of you and mention you in our prayers, constantly remembering before our God and Father your work of faith and labor of love and steadfastness of hope in our Lord Jesus Christ. For we know, brothers and sisters beloved by God, that he has chosen you, because our message of the gospel came to you not in word only, but also in power and in the Holy Spirit and with full conviction (I Thessalonians 1:1-5a).

It is the responsibility of vital leaders to help congregations be *shaped* by the vision of God's love in Jesus and the mission of *sharing* God's love in Jesus. The foundation that allows Christian transformational leaders to accomplish this responsibility of vital leadership is their relationship with the congregation. The church of the Thessalonians was shaped by its relationship with its founders—Paul, Silvanus, and Timothy. One of the earliest Epistles of the New Testament, The First Letter of Paul to the Thessalonians was written to followers of Jesus who were living in Thessalonica, a gateway city to Rome's eastern colonies. In the context of this reality, Acts 17:1-14 records the challenges Paul, Silas (identified as Silvanus in I Thessalonians), and Timothy encountered in sharing the vision of God's love in Jesus with people whose lives had been influenced by the multiplicity of cultures and religions that intersected in Thessalonica—much like the cultural reality in many communities today. In spite of these challenges that were manifested in the form of persecution, a congregation was formed. It was to this congregation that I Thessalonians was written. Key to this letter is Paul's acknowledgement of the relationship that Paul, Silvanus, and Timothy had with this community of faith. It was because of this relationship that Paul sent Timothy to strengthen and encourage the Thessalonians:

> Therefore when we could bear it no longer, we decided to be left alone in Athens; and we sent Timothy, our brother and co-worker for God in proclaiming the gospel of Christ, to strengthen and encourage you for the sake of your faith, so that no one would be shaken by these persecutions. Indeed, you yourselves know that this is what we are destined for. In fact, when we were with you, we told you beforehand that we were to suffer persecution; so it turned out, as you know. For this reason, when I could bear it no longer, I sent to find out about your faith; I was afraid that somehow the tempter had tempted you and that our labor had been in vain.
>
> But Timothy has just now come to us from you, and has brought us the good news of your faith and love. He has told us also that you always remember us kindly and long to see us—just as we long to see you. For this reason, brothers and sisters, during all our distress and persecution we have been encouraged about you through your faith (I Thessalonians 3:1-7).

Because of his love for the Thessalonians, Paul sent Timothy to encourage the members of this congregation to be vitally strong in their faith. In fulfilling this responsibility, Timothy exhorted the church of the Thessalonians to live in the vision and mission of God's love in Jesus that had formed this congregation. Strengthening and encouraging them to be strong in their faith, Timothy accomplished the responsibility of a Christian vital leader. In receiving Timothy's report regarding the Thessalonians, Paul reported of his encouragement through their faith.

The *Book of Discipline* states the importance of vital leadership in helping congregations to be strengthened and encouraged in their faith.

> The privilege of servant leadership in the Church is the call to share in the preparation of congregations and the whole Church for the mission of God in the world. The obligation of servant leadership is the forming of Christian disciples in the covenant community of the congregation. This involves discerning and nurturing the spiritual relationship with God that is the privilege of all servant ministers. It also involves instructing and guiding Christian disciples in their witness to Jesus Christ in the world through acts of worship, devotion, compassion, and justice under the guidance of the Holy Spirit. John Wesley described this as "watching over one another in love."[4]

Lay servants are integral to the mission that has focused the Wesleyan movement since it first began with John Wesley—making disciples of Jesus Christ. The United Methodist Church has assigned specific responsibilities for certified lay servants in the role of servant leadership:

> The certified lay servant serves the local church or charge (or beyond the local church or charge) in ways in which his or her witness, leadership, and service inspires

others to a deeper commitment to Christ and more effective discipleship.[5]

Charged with the goal of inspiring the laity of a local church to "deeper commitment to Christ and more effective discipleship," lay servants who are Christian transformational leaders seek to influence the behavior and actions of a local church through their own commitment to Christ and their own discipleship. The desired outcome of their ministry is a congregation that is transformed in its commitment to Christ and discipleship. The *Discipline* details how all lay servants are able to accomplish the responsibilities of their ministry through the context of their Christian communities:

> The certified lay servant, through continued study and training, should prepare to undertake one or more of the following functions, giving primary attention to service within the local church or charge, United Methodist collegiate ministry, or other United Methodist ministry setting:
>
> - Provide leadership, assistance, and support to the program emphases of the church or other United Methodist ministry.
> - Lead meetings for prayer, training, study, and discussion when requested by the pastor, district superintendent, or committee on Lay Servant Ministries.
> - Conduct, or assist in conducting, services of worship, preach the Word, or give addresses when requested by the pastor, district superintendent, or committee on Lay Servant Ministries.

- Work with appropriate committees and teams which provide congregational and community life or foster caring ministries.
- Assist in the distribution of the elements of Holy Communion upon request by a pastor.
- Teach the Scriptures, doctrine, organization, and ministries of The United Methodist Church.[6]

Christian transformational leaders understand that the fulfillment of these duties is not a list to be checked off, but actions that move a congregation toward vitality.

Lay servants seek to influence the behavior and actions of a local church through their own commitment to Christ and their own discipleship.

It is the role of leaders to be stewards of the vision and mission of the congregation. Leaders hold the congregation accountable for aligning behaviors and actions with mission and vision. Christian transformational leaders accomplish this role through the disciplines of faithful remembering, faithful equipping, and faithful encouraging.

When a congregation finds itself wandering in search of vision and mission, the three disciplines of Christian transformational leadership can help the identity of that congregation be transformed. Priorities and behaviors can be shaped by a renewal of missional purpose. This cannot happen without the influence of Christian transformational leaders who are able to respond to present realities through future trust in God.

A Case in Point—Marc's Story

When I was appointed as a district superintendent, I worked with congregations in envisioning what it meant to be aligned with the mission of making disciples of Jesus Christ. One of the questions I asked as part of the process of visioning was, "Where do you see your congregation in five years?" If leaders of the congregation could not answer that question, I would reframe it by asking, "Where do you see your congregation in two years?" If leaders could not answer that question, I would ask, "Where do you see your congregation in six months?" I found that the answers to these questions told me much about the vitality of congregations. Congregations that were forward looking and had a sense of vision and mission could usually provide ready responses to the questions. Congregations that had no sense of hope were unable to respond. The common factor that I found in a congregation's ability to answer these questions as well as a congregation's inability to answer these questions was based on how they were responding to the ministry settings in which they were located. Congregations that had chosen to respond to their ministry settings through a sense of trust in God's presence within their communities were able to communicate a clearer vision for ministry. Whether they were in a growing community that was reflected in the demographics of their congregation or in a changing community that was reflected in the possibility of new demographics for their congregation, their ministry choices were statements of faith about the presence of

God. Likewise, they realized their ministry decisions were reflections of how they chose to witness to God's presence in their local communities. As communities of Jesus' disciples, they based these ministry decisions on Hebrews 13:8—"Jesus Christ is the same yesterday and today and forever"—as they reflected on how their church had witnessed about Jesus Christ in the past, is witnessing about Jesus Christ in the present, and will witness about Jesus Christ in the future.

——— Questions for Reflection and Discussion ———

1. What does it look like for a vital leader to be in relationship with a congregation?
2. How are vital leaders witnesses of grace and stewards of the vision and mission of their congregation?
3. How can the disciplines of Christian transformational leadership help the identity of a congregation to be transformed?

Part Four: Vital Discipleship

Vital disciples live their lives in accountability with Jesus. To understand the transformative context in which disciples live in accountability with Jesus, we shall review Jesus' appointment of his first disciples to live as a community of faith in Mark 3, the redemption of Jesus' crucifixion in Mark 15, and the resurrected Jesus' invitation to discipleship in Mark 16.

Mark 3:13-19 gives the account of how Jesus appointed his followers to the calling of being his disciples:

He went up the mountain and called to him those whom he wanted, and they came to him. And he appointed twelve, whom he also named apostles, to be with him, and to be sent out to proclaim the message, and to have authority to cast out demons. So he appointed the twelve, Simon (to whom he gave the name Peter); James son of Zebedee and John the brother of James (to whom he gave the name Boanerges, that is, Sons of Thunder); and Andrew and Philip, and Bartholomew, and Matthew, and Thomas, and James son of Alphaeus, and Thaddeus, and Simon the Cananaean, and Judas Iscariot, who betrayed him.

Jesus' appointment of the twelve disciples to become a community of his followers was, first of all, an appointment "to be with him." It was within the context of accountable relationship with Jesus that his disciples would understand their relationship together as a community of faith. In turn, through the context of living in relationship with Jesus and one another, they would be empowered to understand the purpose of their calling. To fully understand the context of Jesus' appointment of his first followers in Mark 3:13-19 "to be with him, and to be sent out to proclaim the message, and to have authority to cast out demons," it is necessary to review the preceding verses of Mark 3:7-12:

Jesus departed with his disciples to the sea, and a great multitude from Galilee followed him; hearing all that he was doing, they came to him in great numbers from Judea, Jerusalem, Idumea, beyond the Jordan, and the region around Tyre and Sidon. He told his disciples to have a boat ready for him because of the crowd, so that they would not crush him; for he had cured many, so that all who had diseases pressed upon him to touch him. Whenever the unclean spirits saw him, they fell down before him and shouted, "You are the Son of God!" But he sternly ordered them not to make him known.

In these verses that precede Jesus' appointment of his disciples to become a community of faith, it is important to note that the disciples were already following Jesus as he departed with them to the sea and told them to have a boat ready for him. While the disciples had responded to Jesus' call to follow him (as witnessed in the call stories of Simon, Andrew, James, and John in Mark 1:16-20 and Levi in Mark 2:13-18), Jesus had not yet appointed them to become a community of his followers. Equally as important is Jesus' interaction with the unclean spirits as they shouted, "You are the Son of God." Mark reports that Jesus "sternly ordered them not to make him known." While the unclean spirits, or demons, were correct in understanding the identity of Jesus, their proclamation of his identity was not concerned with the right relationship that Jesus as the "Son of God" made possible. To understand the right relationship with God that Jesus made possible as the "Son of God," Jesus appointed twelve disciples to live with him as a community of faith in Mark 3:14. Living in relationship as a community of faith, they often did not fully comprehend Jesus' identity, what Jesus was teaching, or where Jesus was leading. Still, they followed Jesus through the hope of answering his call upon their lives. Ultimately, this journey of answering God's call would lead them from the mountain where they were first appointed to life as a community of Jesus' followers to the hill of Calvary where Jesus' true identity as the Son of God would be revealed in Mark 15:33-39:

> When it was noon, darkness came over the whole land until three in the afternoon. At three o'clock Jesus cried out with a loud voice, "Eloi, Eloi, lema sabachthani?" which means, "My God, my God, why have you forsaken me?" When some of the bystanders heard it, they said, "Listen, he is calling for Elijah." And someone ran, filled a sponge with sour wine, put it on a stick, and gave it to him to drink, saying, "Wait, let us see whether Elijah will come to take him down." Then Jesus gave a loud cry and breathed his last. And the curtain of the temple was torn in two, from top to bottom. Now when the centurion, who stood facing him, saw that in this way he breathed his last, he said, "Truly this man was God's Son!"

When Jesus appointed his disciples to become a community of faith in Mark 3, the purpose of their life together was to:

- be with Jesus so they might understand his true identity by living in relationship with him and with one another.
- proclaim the message of right relationship with God through Jesus.
- have authority over the powers that seek to destroy right relationship with God.

Called to this purpose as a community of faith, they would eventually understand Jesus' identity and the purpose of their life together through the cross. The crucifixion account in Mark 15 tells how the full identity of Jesus was revealed to the community of his disciples as he restored right relationship with God through his death. In Mark 15:38, the evidence of right relationship being restored was shown through the tearing in two of the curtain of the temple (a symbol of separation from God) as Jesus died on the cross. The crucifixion also witnesses to the true identity of Jesus as the centurion proclaimed, "Truly this man was God's Son."

The story and responsibility of discipleship, however, does not end with the crucifixion of Jesus in Mark 15. It continues with the resurrection account of Jesus in Mark 16:1-7 as Mary Magdalene, Mary the mother of James, and Salome went to the tomb for the purpose of anointing Jesus' body.

When the Sabbath was over, Mary Magdalene, and Mary the mother of James, and Salome bought spices, so that they might go and anoint him. And very early on the first day of the week, when the sun had risen, they went to the tomb. They had been saying to one another, "Who will roll away the stone for us from the entrance to the tomb?" When they looked up, they saw that the stone, which was very large, had already been rolled back. As they entered the tomb, they saw a young man, dressed in a white robe, sitting on the right side; and they were alarmed. But he said to them, "Do not be alarmed; you are looking for Jesus of Nazareth, who was crucified. He has been raised; he is not here. Look, there is the place they laid him. But go, tell his disciples and Peter that he is going ahead of you to Galilee; there you will see him, just as he told you."

The message the women received at the empty tomb was a message that Jesus' invitation to discipleship did not end with his crucifixion. To the contrary, the responsibility of being with Jesus by living in relationship with Jesus and one another, proclaiming right relationship with God through Jesus, and having authority over powers that seek to destroy right relationship with God was empowered through the cross and the empty tomb. The women were given the apostolic responsibility of telling this resurrection story to the disciples whom Jesus had appointed to be a community of faith. Key to this resurrection account is the fact that the risen Lord would be waiting for the disciples in Galilee—the place where Jesus first appointed his disciples to be a community of faith.

The resurrected Christ still appoints his disciples to live as communities of faith who are accountable in relationship with him, who proclaim the message of right relationship with God, and who have authority over the powers that seek to destroy right relationship with God. As communities of Jesus' disciples live into this calling, they become vital congregations that help transform the world.

A Case in Point—John's Story

It is often said in the church that there is a vast difference between knowing about Jesus and knowing Jesus. Any student of history can know about the historical Jesus; however, followers of Jesus know him as their redeemer, their model and companion for living. Followers of Jesus do not simply affirm the life, death, and resurrection of Jesus, they become actively engaged in their faith and Jesus' call to discipleship.

One of my former parishioners shared his call to vital discipleship. George was in his late forties when we first met. He explained that his parents had raised him in the church. From his earliest memories, he attended Sunday school and worship every Sunday. Throughout his childhood, he participated in his church's activities for children and youth. Then, he went to college where he was not quite so diligent about his faith. It wasn't long before he stopped going to church. After college, this pattern continued. He reasoned he knew about Jesus; he was a Christian. He did not believe that it was necessary to be engaged in a church congregation. In fact, one Sunday a friend quipped that "he could worship God in the beauty of a golf course just as well as in church."

When George married, he returned to the church, and as his children were born he became an active participant once again. He even began to take on some leadership roles. As a successful business owner, he was quite comfortable taking on leadership responsibilities. Although George enjoyed his new relationship with the church, he began to have a feeling of emptiness. It became obvious that his affluent lifestyle was not providing him the fulfillment he had hoped for and expected. He didn't understand why. He had all the things in life he could want. Yet, his life was unfulfilled. George said that he began a period of reflection and discernment during his late thirties because of his "feeling of emptiness."

He shared that one day while in prayer, he remembered the passage from Matthew 7:7-8, "Ask, and it will be given you; search, and you will find; knock, and the door will be opened for you. For everyone who asks receives, and everyone who searches finds, and for everyone who knocks, the door will be opened." In desperation, he asked for God to show him the way to a life of fulfillment. He said for the first time in his life, he sought to know the living Christ. He was knocking.

George recognized that he had not been following the practices of discipleship. He began reading his Bible and joined several small-group Bible studies that resulted in the development of a deeper and more personal relationship with his living Lord. In time, he understood that, although he was raised in a church family, his sense of emptiness came from having only a secular knowledge of Jesus. Realizing that fulfillment in life comes as grace from God, he became a disciple of the living Christ. In short, he experienced the transforming grace of God and the joy of vital discipleship.

Over the next several years, George began a men's Bible study that continues to this day. He initiated a Stephen's Ministry and participated in many other activities that encouraged others in their faith. George did indeed become a vital disciple as he lived his life in relationship with the living Lord.

──── Questions for Reflection and Discussion ────

1. Why is it important for a Christian transformational leader to be engaged as a vital disciple?

2. What are examples of "powers" that seek to destroy right relationship with God and hinder congregational vitality?

3. Why does Jesus appoint his disciples to live as a community of faith?

Part Five: Vital Alignment

Alignment is the process of moving an organization in a shared direction for a shared cause. Alignment does not mean that people within the organization will always agree with one another as they move forward. Alignment does mean they will remain in community with one another as they discern the best way to move forward together. Over time, as people share in the common vision, behaviors and actions will begin to weave together in a tapestry of transformation.

Congregations are vital when they are aligned toward the vision of life that God has cast through Jesus. The apostle Paul shared his vision of congregational life in Philippians 2:1-4:

> If then there is any encouragement in Christ, any consolation from love, any sharing in the Spirit, any compassion and sympathy, make my joy complete: be of the same mind, having the same love, being in full accord and of one mind. Do nothing from selfish ambition or conceit, but in humility regard others as better than yourselves. Let each of you look not to your own interests, but to the interests of others.

To fully appreciate Paul's vision of congregational life, it is necessary to realize some of the factors the Philippian church was facing. First, this congregation was the initial church that Paul had begun on European soil. Second, the Philippian congregation was formed by people who did not agree with one another. Third, Paul wrote this letter from his prison cell because he had been faithful to the gospel of Christ. Fourth, there were some people in the Philippian congregation who had used Paul's imprisonment to advance their own agendas. It is in the reality of these factors that Paul began his letter to the Philippian congregation with these words found in Philippians 1:3-11:

> I thank my God every time I remember you, constantly praying with joy in every one of my prayers for all of you, because of your sharing in the gospel from the first day until now. I am confident of this, that the one who began a good work among you will bring it to completion by the day of Jesus Christ. It is right for me to think this way about all of you, because you hold me in your heart for all of you share in God's grace with me, both in my imprisonment and in the defense and confirmation of the gospel. For God is my witness, how I long for all of you with the compassion of Christ Jesus. And this is my prayer, that your love may overflow more and more with knowledge and full insight to help you to determine what is best, so that in the day of Christ you may be pure and blameless, having produced the harvest of righteousness that comes through Jesus Christ for the glory and praise of God.

What allowed Paul to write with such affection to a congregation that was formed by people of differing opinions and agendas?

Writing from his prison cell, Paul was practicing the disciplines of Christian transformational leadership as he faithfully remembered the partnership of the Philippian congregation, faithfully sought to equip them through his epistle, and faithfully encouraged them to live in the vision of who God was calling them to become as followers of Jesus: a congregation measured by the vitality of God's grace and the harvest of righteousness that comes through Jesus Christ for the glory and praise of God.

Alignment is the process of moving an organization in a shared direction for a shared cause.

The factors that empowered Paul's vision of congregational vitality were:

- The ways the Philippian congregation had shared in God's grace with him from the beginning of his ministry with them and how that grace was being shared with him in his current imprisonment;
- His prayer that the congregation would allow their love to overflow with knowledge and full insight;
- His hope that the Philippian congregation would produce the harvest of righteousness that comes through Jesus Christ for the glory and praise of God.

Guided by a vision of the gospel of Jesus Christ that looked beyond the current circumstances of his imprisonment, Paul invited the Philippians to align themselves beyond the current circumstances that defined their congregation so they might "produce the harvest of righteousness that comes through Jesus Christ for the glory and praise of God." If they would be able to align themselves to this vision, then they would be vital in their ministry and witness.

Paul began his letter to the people who formed the Philippian church by reminding them of the accountability of their partnership in ministry with him. Twice he reminds the congregation "of your sharing the gospel from the first day until now" and how they continued to share in God's grace with him in his "imprisonment and in the defense and confirmation of the gospel." Faithful in his personal accountability for sharing the message of the gospel of Jesus Christ, Paul was reminding the members of the Philippian church of the personal accountability of their ministry as a congregation. It was the vision of this foundational calling that allowed Paul to write with joy from a prison cell. Even though some people within the Philippian congregation sought to use Paul's imprisonment as a means to discredit his ministry, Paul rejoiced because of the partnership in the message of the gospel of Jesus Christ that he had experienced in forming this congregation. Now, he was writing in the certainty that the same partnership in the message of the gospel of Jesus Christ that had formed the Philippian church could transform it, even in the midst of inner dissension. Casting a vision of congregational life that focused beyond the dissension being experienced in this congregation, Paul wrote of a future that had not yet been fully realized. Understanding that congregational behavior and actions can be either signposts of hope or signposts of hopelessness, Paul realized that vitality is measured by God's grace and "the harvest of righteousness that comes through Jesus Christ for the glory and praise of God."

Even though the Philippian congregation had recently begun, it was facing a critical moment of alignment as it discerned its identity and calling as a community of faith. At some point in its existence, every congregation must respond to critical questions about its identity and calling as it determines how it is aligned with its vision and mission.

If a congregation is going to align itself with the vision of loving God and the mission of sharing God's love through Jesus, then it must be willing to make vital decisions about how it will be accountable to God's vision of love as revealed through the life, death, and resurrection of Jesus. These decisions require a congregation to align itself with the mission of redemption. As a community of Christian disciples becomes accountable in its relationship with Jesus, proclaims and lives the message of right relationship with God, and takes authority over the powers that seek to destroy right relationship with God, it becomes a vital congregation.

In a congregation, as with any organization that has many people and ideas, programs must be periodically evaluated and adjusted to ensure consistent alignment with the organization's goals. This "alignment adjustment" takes stock of whether a congregation's efforts are moving in the direction of its mission. Some congregations do this when they discern a new mission; others do this on a regular schedule. A simple process for conducting an "alignment adjustment" is to list all the efforts of the congregation (classes, mission projects, ministries, events, etc.) and then ask these three questions:

What must we KEEP doing to accomplish our mission?

What must we STOP doing that is not aligned with our mission?

What must we START doing to achieve our mission?

In answering these questions, it is important to note that there are no bad efforts. Rather, the concept to consider is one of stewardship. Which efforts offer the highest and best use of the resources God has given us?

—— Questions for Reflection and Discussion ——

1. What does it mean for a congregation to align with Jesus' vision and mission?

2. Why is it important for a congregation to periodically conduct an "alignment adjustment"?

3. What are the differences between alignment and agreement? Does everyone in a church need to agree for a church to move forward?

CHAPTER FOUR

Assessing a Congregation's Current Reality

Part One: Defining Current Reality

Any organization that seeks to increase its effectiveness must first understand its current reality. What are the components of a congregation's current reality? How can Christian transformational leaders help their congregations discern and build upon the foundation of their current reality? The first step in a congregation's transformation is to engage in an intentional process that defines its current reality.

From a congregation's beginning, its history is formed as it is organized to witness to Christ's presence in the world. Over time, as a congregation responds to this founding call by making decisions and experiencing results, a congregational culture is formed. Each year, a new layer of identity is either added or reinforced toward this culture. Christian transformational leaders realize that congregational identity and culture may strengthen or hinder their leadership. To lead a movement of transformation, they help their congregations understand who they are as followers of Jesus and what they are called to do.

A Congregation's Current Reality

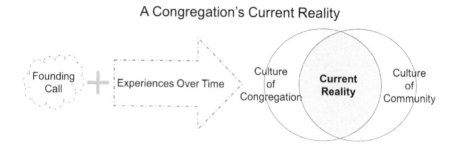

A congregation's current reality may be defined as the combination of history and future possibilities through which the congregational culture intersects with the community culture. Every congregation has a current reality through which congregants live out their call to discipleship. Some of the more important layers that influence current reality include the congregation's understanding of its mission, the demographics of the surrounding community, and the ways people within the congregation interact with one another and with the neighboring community.

The gospels of Matthew, Mark, Luke, and John tell the story of Jesus' interactions with his followers, religious leaders, and others. In Matthew 23:1-12, Jesus defines the current reality of many of the religious leaders of the time:

> Then Jesus said to the crowds and to his disciples, "The scribes and the Pharisees sit on Moses' seat; therefore, do whatever they teach you and follow it; but do not do as they do, for they do not practice what they teach. They tie up heavy burdens, hard to bear and lay them on the shoulders

of others; but they themselves are unwilling to lift a finger to move them. They do all their deeds to be seen by others; for they make their phylacteries broad and their fringes long. They love to have the place of honor at banquets and the best seats in the synagogues, and to be greeted with respect in the marketplaces, and to have people call them rabbi. But you are not to be called rabbi, for you have one teacher, and you are all students. And call no one your father on earth, for you have one Father—the one in heaven. Nor are you to be called instructors, for you have one instructor, the Messiah. The greatest among you will be your servant. All who exalt themselves will be humbled, and all who humble themselves will be exalted."

Jesus' description of the scribes and Pharisees is an accurate depiction of the current reality that defined many of the religious leaders of his time. Jesus draws a sharp contrast between this current reality and his understanding of discipleship by teaching the new reality of servanthood: "The greatest among you will be your servant." It is this new reality that leads to transformational discipleship and becomes the lens through which followers of Jesus assess how they are following their Savior.

—— Questions for Reflection and Discussion ——

1. Why is it important to understand the current reality of a congregation?
2. How did Jesus assess current reality through the reality of servanthood?

3. Why is engagement in an intentional process that defines current reality the first step in a congregation's transformation?

Part Two: Assessing Current Reality

Transformational leaders assess current reality through the lens of Jesus' vision of servanthood.

Current reality should be assessed through the lens of a desired new reality. Christian transformational leaders assess current reality through the lens of Jesus' vision of servanthood as they look at the past, present, and future. Most organizational assessments of current reality fall into three basic categories:

- In what environment do we find ourselves?
  - What were the original objectives and expectations of the church's founding call?
  - What is the history of this congregation?
  - What factors have led to the present composition of this congregation?
- What are the facts about our present state?
  - How does the leadership engage and encourage the faith of its worshiping community; i.e., number of Bible studies, discipleship groups, etc.
  - What is the makeup of the congregation? (age, gender, family composition, ethnicity, strengths and needs, etc.)

- What is the makeup of the surrounding community, (age, gender, family composition, ethnicity, strengths and needs, etc.)
- What is important to us about our future?
  - What are the most pressing issues facing the future of the congregation?
  - What are the most pressing issues facing the future of the community?
  - How is God calling this congregation to love its neighbor?

The assessment of a congregation is first and foremost a spiritual endeavor. Congregational assessment is not simply a matter of reviewing numbers or statistical data, although these are important tools for measuring the current reality of a congregation. Understanding that statistics can provide insight about congregational vitality, Christian transformational leaders interpret these numbers through the framework of discipleship and the evidence of transformation not only in their congregations but also in the corner of the world where their congregations are located.

The assessment of a congregation is first and foremost a spiritual endeavor.

A spiritual means for assessing the current reality of a congregation is found in the Lord's Prayer. Matthew 6:9-13 and Luke 11:2-4 record the prayer that Jesus taught his disciples when they asked him to teach them how to pray. Matthew's version of Jesus' prayer will provide the context for the spiritual assessment of vitality that will be discerned in this chapter:

> Our Father in heaven, hallowed be your name. Your kingdom come. Your will be done, on earth as it is in heaven. Give us this day our daily bread. And forgive us our debts, as we also have forgiven our debtors. And do not bring us to the time of trial, but rescue us from the evil one (Matthew 6:9-13).

Christian transformational leaders assess the current reality of a congregation by listening for the ways that Jesus' prayer is heard in the life of a congregation. In what ways does the narrative of congregational life hallow or honor God's name? In what ways is that congregation a sign of God's kingdom coming on earth and God's will being done on earth as it is in heaven? In what ways does that congregation connect people to the gift of God's grace that provides strength for living through the daily sustenance of God's presence? In what ways are members of that congregation living in the holy reciprocity of forgiveness? In what ways is that congregation clinging to and embracing the presence of God? In what ways is that congregation connecting people to the prayer that Jesus taught his disciples to pray? Knowing that the answers to these questions provides the context for assessing the vitality of a congregation, Christian transformational leaders review how congregational values, resources, and behaviors align with the prayer that Jesus taught. They accomplish this responsibility by:

- listening to the language used in a congregation,
- understanding the tribes or subgroups that constitute a congregation,

- assessing community demographics,
- assessing congregational patterns,
- receiving congregational input,
- processing information.

Acts 6:1-7 gives the account of the apostles' assessment of the current reality facing the early church and their response to this reality.

> Now during those days, when the disciples were increasing in number, the Hellenists complained against the Hebrews because their widows were being neglected in the daily distribution of food. And the twelve called together the whole community of the disciples and said, "It is not right that we should neglect the word of God in order to wait on tables. Therefore, friends, select from among yourselves seven men of good standing, full of the Spirit and of wisdom, whom we may appoint to this task, while we, for our part, will devote ourselves to prayer and to serving the word." What they said pleased the whole community, and they chose Stephen, a man full of faith and the Holy Spirit, together with Philip, Prochorus, Nicanor, Timon, Parmenas, and Nicolaus, a proselyte of Antioch. They had these men stand before the apostles, who prayed and laid their hands on them. The word of God continued to spread; the number of the disciples increased greatly in Jerusalem, and a great many of the priests became obedient to the faith.

Assessing the current reality of the early church, the apostles listened to the language being used, understood the makeup and needs of the congregation, received congregational input, and acted accordingly as they faithfully remembered the mission to which they were called.

Listening to the language being used in a congregation—Language in vital congregations is oriented toward the goal of God's kingdom being realized and God's will being done on earth as it is in heaven. Living in the understanding that true transformation of the world will occur only as God's kingdom is realized on earth, the language of vital congregations is shaped by the possibility of transformation. The language of vitality is shaped by the vision of what a transformed world will look like because of the ministry of that congregation. The congregation would ask such questions as—"What would it look like if . . . ?"; "Where is God calling us to . . . ?"; "How is God calling our congregation to connect with our community and the world?"

The language of vitality is not a denial of past reality nor an avoidance of present reality. Instead, it is an acknowledgement of God's faithfulness, as a congregation embraces the challenges and possibilities before it. The language of vitality is a confession of faith that affirms the daily gift of God's sustaining presence. The language of vitality hallows God's name when the ministry of a congregation connects followers of Jesus to the prayer that Jesus taught his disciples.

Murmuring is the word that describes life in churches that allow fears of the present and future to be coupled with a desire to cling to the past.

When followers of Jesus are not connected to the prayer that Jesus taught, murmuring can define the current reality of a congregation. Murmuring is heard when the fear of the unknown is coupled with the desire to cling to the past. Murmuring is heard in the story of Israel following the Exodus when the former slaves of Egypt encountered the challenges of living into a new identity of freedom. Exodus 15:24 records the first biblical account of murmuring after the slaves of Israel walked to freedom on dry ground through the sea. Three days into their journey of freedom, they encountered nondrinkable water. Facing this challenge, the people murmured against their leader, Moses. The Participant's Workbook for *Does Your Church Have a Prayer? In Mission Toward the Promised Land* defines the way murmuring is heard in the life of congregations:

> Murmuring is the word that describes life in churches that allow fears of the present and future to be coupled with a desire to cling to the past. In these congregations, murmuring may be heard in church hallways, in Sunday school classes, in parking lots after church meetings, in telephone conversations, and in emails. The topic of murmuring is often disappointment with the perception of a church's present ministry. In murmuring congregations, people often identify the pastor or different church entities as the cause of the problem. "Us," "them," and "you people" color the language in murmuring congregations. Questions in murmuring congregations tend to focus more on fear of the future than hope for the future. In the vocabulary

of murmuring, the past tense is heard more often than the future tense.[1]

Every congregation has different constituencies or tribes that affect its life and ministry.

Christian transformational leaders listen for the language they hear in the everyday life of their church when they assess a congregation's vitality. They also listen to the types of languages that are being spoken in a congregation.

Understanding the tribes that constitute a congregation—Every congregation has different constituencies or tribes that affect its life and ministry. Christian transformational leaders understand the reality of these tribes as they assess current reality and lead congregational change. Representing different values and voices in a local church, congregational tribes respond to the past, present, and future life of that congregation. Christian transformational leaders understand that it is important for all tribes or voices to be recognized. Leading into a transformed future, they realize the voice of each tribe needs to be heard since the tribes may give permission or opposition to ministry plans. Instead of interpreting the tribes as competitors for the church's vision, leaders understand the importance of hearing each voice as it influences the present and future directions of the congregation. Some of the tribes that may be present in a congregation are:

The Tribe of the Good Old Days—This tribe is primarily concerned with preserving the memories of the perceived past glory days of a congregation. It sees the church as a place that harbors the security of past memories in the midst of a changing world. While this tribe is not opposed to new people in the church, it believes that new people's primary role is to support the present ministry structure and not rock the boat. We hear the voice of this tribe through such statements as: "I remember when our pews used to be filled and our Sunday school rooms were overflowing with children" and "Why can't we do things like we used to?"

The Tribe of Forgetting the Past—This tribe is primarily concerned with the future without understanding how the history of the church affects present and future ministry. This tribe sees tradition as a roadblock to the future. Its members cherish their roles of rocking the boat. The voice of this tribe is heard through such statements as: "The past is the past. Let's move on" and "Times have changed."

The Tribe of Control—This tribe is primarily concerned with power. Members of this tribe believe they are responsible for running the church. Within this tribe, preservation of control is a primary concern, even though the language of the tribe is cloaked in words of concern for the overall life of the church. This tribe sees its role as preserving the church for future generations, often at the expense of the present generation. The voice of this tribe is heard through such statements as: "I am responsible for this ministry"; "This is my job"; "You don't understand."

The Tribe of Spiritual Elitism—This tribe is concerned with judging the spiritual vitality of the congregation by its own values of faith. Members of this tribe are defined by their adherence to specific doctrinal beliefs that give security to their lives or by personal experiences that give validity to their expressions of faith. This tribe believes it is responsible for determining the credibility of other people's leadership by its self-imposed standards of spirituality. The voice of this tribe is heard through such statements as "You'll understand one day" and "God will make it clear to you."

The Tribe of Business Values—This tribe is concerned with judging the vitality of the church by its own values of business life. Members of this tribe are defined by their adherence to specific business practices that give security to their businesses. This tribe believes that the church must be run like a business if it is going to survive. The voice of this tribe is heard through such statements as "We need to run the church like a business" and "What's the bottom line?"

The Tribe of Apathy—This tribe tries to appear unconcerned. Members of this tribe care about the church, but they have detached themselves from voicing an opinion because they realize they are not valued by the other tribes within the church. This tribe believes the church can survive with them or without them. The voice of this tribe is heard through such statements as "Whatever"; "Don't ask me"; "Do you really want to know?"

The Tribe of Remembering Encouragers—This tribe believes the church exists for one reason: to glorify God. Members of this tribe care about the church, understand the importance of *faithful remembering*, and persist in their faith. They are concerned with helping their congregation live into the promise of God's faithfulness. The voice of this tribe is heard through such statements as: "I hear what you are saying"; "God is with us"; "I really want to know"; "Why haven't we done it that way before?" "Where is God calling us as a community of faith?" "How can we move forward together?"[2]

Christian transformational leaders are members of the Tribe of Remembering Encouragers. They assess the current reality of their congregations by connecting the story of their congregation's life to the larger story of God's faithfulness. Speaking the language of hope, they focus on helping the tribes of their congregation see how their values connect to the value of God's kingdom coming on earth and God's will being done on earth as it is in heaven. Their focus is to help the tribes of their congregation see beyond their individual concerns as they listen for God's voice and ask how they can work together in responding to the questions that are facing their congregations.

A Case in Point—John's Story

A congregation I worked with as a consultant was established in the 1930s as a neighborhood church in an affluent section of a large metropolitan city. Membership grew significantly for the first fifty years of its existence, and it was recognized as one of the most affluent and influential churches in the city. In the 1980s, however, suburban sprawl began to affect its membership and worshiping community. Over the next thirty years, this once-thriving church became inwardly focused, as the once-affluent neighborhood was changing. Property values were declining, and a new community was emerging. Within the congregation were two approaches to deal with this new reality. One group remembered the history and glory of this church as it focused on the past. Another group recognized the

Tribe of the Good Old Days	Tribe of Spiritual Elitism
"I remember when our pews used to be filled and our Sunday school rooms were overflowing with children." "Why can't we do things like we used to?"	"You'll understand one day." "God will make it clear to you."
Tribe of Forgetting the Past	Tribe of Business Values
"The past is the past. Let's move on." "Times have changed."	"We need to run the church like a business." "What's the bottom line?"
Tribe of Control	Tribe of Apathy
"I am responsible for this ministry." "This is my job." "You don't understand."	"Whatever." "Don't ask me." "Do you really want to know?"
Tribe of Remembering Encouragers "I hear what you are saying." "God is with us." "I really want to know." "Why haven't we done it that way before?" "Where is God calling us as a community of faith?" "How can we move forward together?"	

importance of ministry to the new community. They embraced Jesus' command to "love your neighbor as yourself." They began to discuss what love of neighbor and neighborhood would look like. Opening their doors to the community, they began to connect with community organizations and listen to community concerns. This new level of relationship allowed the congregation to move from personal, internal concerns to community concerns. It was not an easy journey, but over time, the church became a relevant presence in the neighborhood.

One of the major questions facing a local congregation is relevancy.

Assessing community demographics—One of the major questions facing a local congregation is relevancy. The answer to the question of relevancy will be determined by the ways congregations choose to respond to the strengths and challenges of their communities. What are the characteristics of the current population as represented by age, race, education, marriage, families, and religious preferences? What major concerns do people within the community face?

Congregations that choose to live in relationship with their communities adapt to the realities of their communities as they are guided by Jesus' teaching about loving God and loving neighbor. Some congregations choose to live in denial about the realities of their communities. Fearful of the future, they cling to the past. Longing for the days when their communities were defined by different demographic realities, they avoid questions of relevancy for the people of their current community. Conversations in these congregations turn inward as they choose not to live in relationship with their communities. In turn, the story of those congregations becomes a story of isolation from their neighbors as they seek to defend their congregations against the present and the future. Questions about survival rather than questions about mission begin to dominate conversations, and the language of murmuring undermines the language of hope. Rather than embracing or denying the realities of their communities, they make assumptions about their ministries based on partial understandings.

A Case in Point—Kathy's Story

A small church was struggling with what ministries would be most helpful for the people of the community. Church members were willing to engage in almost any ministry that would be relevant. As they discussed this, several members indicated that the community was receiving an influx of non-English speaking Hispanic families. The conclusion was that an English as a Second Language (ESL) program would be helpful, so church members set about developing such a program and advertised it in the community. There were few participants in the program, resulting in the organizers' surprise at the low turnout. They reevaluated the program, re-advertised it, and got the same result. At this point, an external consultant researched and analyzed the demographic data for the community, but the consultant did not see the trends the congregation had forecasted. He asked, "Why did you believe that so many Hispanic families were moving into the community?" As leaders pondered this, they realized that they had acted on anecdotal evidence. Several members had met new Hispanic families and determined that this was a trend. At least, they now knew why the participation in the ESL program was not significant.

The church leaders learned a lot about how best to get to know their community and to develop programs that were relevant for their neighbors. As they dug into the demographic data, they found something that did not make sense on the surface. The data showed that the community was aging and that the number of retirees was rising significantly. But the church's preschool enrollment was climbing. So church leaders set out to find out what was going on. They observed and talked to people as they dropped off children at preschool and found that, in many cases, the retired grandparents were caring for the children and bringing them to preschool.

Their next step was to talk to some of the grandparents and find out about their interests, challenges, and activities. Based on that information, the congregation formed three new small groups that met during preschool hours once per week. The first was a discussion group on caring for grandchildren in today's society. The second was a Bible study. The third was a handyman group whose members used their skills to work on the facility maintenance list for the church. They painted, cleaned, organized, landscaped, and even did some electrical and plumbing work.

Over time, some of those folks began to attend church as well. Most importantly, the church had figured out a way to know their neighbors and be relevant in their lives. As new families signed up for preschool from year to year, the congregation got to know those families as well. It is important for a church to know its community before launching programs that seem relevant, but may not be so.

Vitality can become reality, even when congregations find themselves in the midst of changing communities. Fearful misperceptions about neighbors can be replaced by the love of neighbor. Faith in the daily bread of God's presence can define the reality of a congregation even when that congregation has entered a time of spiritual famine. Congregations can be relevant to the needs of their communities. To lead congregations into relevancy, Christian transformational leaders must assess current congregational realities.

Assessing congregational patterns—Congregational patterns provide a glimpse into the ongoing narrative of a congregation's life. Within The United Methodist Church, there are many methods by which congregational patterns are reported. Year-end reports for each congregation include information about membership, attendance, giving, property, and so on. In addition, a denominational resource called VitalSigns dashboard (see page 63) provides a method for congregations to record average weekly attendance, professions of faith, small groups, mission, and dollars given to mission. While information gathered through annual and weekly reports provides important data for understanding both the historical and present context of a congregation's health, numbers without interpretation are simply numbers. Christian transformational leaders understand the importance of interpreting congregational patterns by assessing how their church is making disciples of Jesus Christ for the transformation of the world. In addition to gathering statistical information (quantitative data), they also gather stories about the missional difference their congregation is making (qualitative data).

Receiving congregational input—Using quantitative and qualitative data, Christian transformational leaders assess how their congregation is telling the story of God's love through Jesus Christ. Some questions that may shape their assessment of congregational reality are: "How are ministries aligned with mission? Are congregational leaders looking for ways to align the actions of the congregation with its vision and mission? What motivates members of the congregation? How has the story of this congregation influenced the story of the surrounding community? What ministry of this congregation had the most significant influence in the surrounding community during the past year? What ministry had the most significant influence in the life of this congregation during the past year? How has this congregation's ministry been a sign of God's kingdom coming and God's will being done on earth as it is in heaven? In what ways does this congregation love God with heart, soul, and mind and its neighbors as itself?" In receiving congregational input, the key value that should guide the assessment process is how that congregation identifies with Jesus' message of servanthood.

The following Scripture passages and questions may be used to assist in the process of receiving congregational input.

Scripture for Reflection

"The greatest among you will be your servant" (Matthew 23:11).

Jesus taught that his followers must be servants. What does it mean to be a servant follower of Jesus?

How is servanthood realized in our church?

Scripture for Reflection

One of the scribes came near and heard them disputing with one another, and seeing that Jesus answered them well, he asked him, "Which commandment is the first of all?" Jesus answered, "The first is, 'Hear, O Israel: the Lord our God, the Lord is one; you shall love the Lord your God with all your heart, and with all your soul, and with all your mind, and with all your strength.' The second is this, 'You shall love your neighbor as yourself.' There is no other commandment greater than these" (Mark 12:28-31).

What does loving God with all our heart, and with all our soul, and with all our mind look like for our church?

What does loving our neighbors as ourselves look like for our church?

Scripture for Reflection

"But strive first for the kingdom of God and his righteousness, and all these things will be given to you as well" (Matthew 6:33).

What does it mean to strive for God's kingdom and God's righteousness?

How is our church striving for God's kingdom and God's righteousness in the present?

What will be required for our church to strive for God's kingdom and God's righteousness in the future?

Scripture for Reflection

"For where your treasure is, there your heart will be also" (Matthew 6:21).

What is treasured at our church? What values define the heart of our church?

Scripture for Reflection

"Where there is no vision, the people perish" (Proverbs 29:18, KJV)

What does vision mean? What is the vision of our church? How does that vision reflect the Great Commandment of Mark 12:28-31?

Scripture for Reflection

If then there is any encouragement in Christ, any consolation from love, any sharing in the Spirit, any compassion and sympathy, make my joy complete: be of the same mind, having the same love, being in full accord and of one mind. Do nothing from selfish ambition or conceit, but in humility regard others as better than yourselves. Let each of you look not to your own interests, but to the interests of others (Philippians 2:1-4).

This Scripture is Paul's vision for the church at Philippi. What are ways this vision can be better realized at our church?

Scripture for Reflection

Let the same mind be in you that was in Christ Jesus, who, though he was in the form of God, did not regard equality with God as something to be exploited, but emptied himself, taking the form of a slave, being born in human likeness. And being found in human form, he humbled himself and became obedient to the point of death—even death on a cross. Therefore God also highly exalted him and gave him the name that is above every name, so that at the name of Jesus every knee should bend, in heaven and on earth and under the earth, and every tongue should confess that Jesus Christ is Lord, to the glory of God the Father (Philippians 2:5-11).

How is the sacrificial servant love of Christ Jesus revealed through our church?

Scripture for Reflection

"Jesus Christ is the same yesterday and today and forever" (Hebrews 13:8).

How has our church witnessed about Jesus Christ in the past? How is our church witnessing about Jesus Christ in the present? How will our church witness about Jesus Christ in the future?

Processing Information

Vital congregations tell the story of God's love through Jesus as they align their vision and mission with the goal of making disciples of Jesus Christ for the transformation of the world. Motivated by love for God and love for neighbor, vital congregations live with faith in the daily gift of God's presence as they trust in God's faithfulness in the future. Signs of God's kingdom coming on earth and God's will being done on earth as it is in heaven are evident as they faithfully remember the story of God's love through Jesus, faithfully equip disciples of Jesus to live the servant story of God's love, and faithfully encourage Christian discipleship through the power of the Holy Spirit. Their current reality is measured by a combination of quantitative and qualitative data that influences present and future ministry decisions. As noted earlier, some of the ways this quantitative and qualitative data is received is by listening to the language being used in a congregation, understanding the tribes that constitute a congregation, assessing community demographics, assessing congregational patterns, and receiving congregational input. It is the responsibility of congregational leaders to process this information so a congregation understands what this information reveals about its current reality:

- What is this information communicating about our congregation's faithfulness to the mission of making disciples of Jesus Christ for the transformation of the world?
- How can this information strengthen the future story of our congregation's faithfulness in making disciples of Jesus Christ for the transformation of the world?

Both the assembling and interpretation of this information should be a combined effort of people who represent different viewpoints of the congregation as future ministry decisions are made based on current congregational realities. It is important that the assessment of a congregation's current reality be as objective as possible so the congregation may trust the integrity of the assessment and make appropriate decisions about current and future ministries.

—— Questions for Reflection and Discussion ——

1. Why is the assessment of a congregation's current reality a spiritual endeavor?
2. How would you assess your congregation's current reality through the Lord's Prayer?

3. How are Christian transformational leaders members of the Tribe of Remembering Encouragers?

Part Three: Congregational Life Stages

All organizations, including congregations, go through life stages. Christian transformational leaders who understand this organizational truth can help their congregations strike the delicate balance that leads to transformation. The life stages of a congregation can be understood as the intersection of chaos and focus.

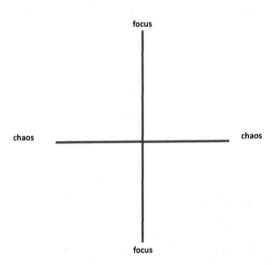

Organizations are naturally chaotic. One of the basic roles of leadership is to bring some sort of order to organizational chaos. Often, leaders believe their role is to end or destroy chaos. But chaos can never be fully avoided, controlled, or destroyed. For transformation to occur, chaos must be embraced, because the essence of creative possibility exists in the chaos. Therefore, Christian transformational leaders must understand the relationship between transformation and creative possibility as they speak order to chaos.

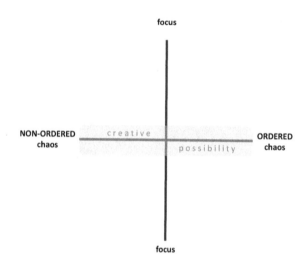

In the beginning when God created the heavens and the earth, the earth was a formless void and darkness covered the face of the deep, while a wind from God swept over the face of the waters (Genesis 1:1-2).

The opening two verses of the Bible affirm two realities:

• The reality of the Creator as defined by the wind of God sweeping over the face of the waters

- The reality of creative possibility as defined by the chaotic formless void of earth and the darkness that covered the face of the deep.

The verses that follow the opening biblical story of creation as found in Genesis 1:3-2:4a tell the story of God speaking order to the creative possibility that is contained in chaos.

As was true in the beginning, the essence of creative possibility is still found in chaotic realities. Just as God embraced the essence of creative possibility, communities of Jesus' disciples are called to embrace the essence of creative possibility as they live in relationship with the God who speaks order to their life together. Affirming their faith in the God of creation and creative possibility, Christian transformational leaders assess a congregation's current reality as they embrace the essence of creative possibility. Key to their assessment is addressing how a congregation is responding to the mission of making disciples of Jesus Christ for the transformation of the world. It is this mission that calls Jesus' followers to align their lives to a vision that is beyond themselves. What is true for individual followers of Jesus is true for communities of Jesus' followers. As congregations are guided by the identity of Jesus, they respond to creative possibilities by focusing beyond themselves. Focus is the second element that shapes the life stages of congregations. Intersecting with creative possibility, focus will either draw congregations beyond self or within self.

Formed by the calling to follow Jesus, vital congregations are guided by an outward focus by embracing the creative realities of chaotic possibilities as they faithfully remember, faithfully equip, and faithfully encourage people to be disciples of Jesus.

> The essence of creative possibility is still found today in chaotic realities.

The reality of congregational life, however, is that sometimes congregations can become inwardly focused as they perform the works of ministry while forgetting their identity. Guided by institutional identity rather than the servant identity of Jesus, they respond to creative possibilities by focusing on themselves. Revelation 2:1-5a contains a vignette of this reality as John addresses the church in Ephesus about the need to keep its focus on Jesus.

To the angel of the church in Ephesus write: These are the words of him who holds the seven stars in his right hand, who walks among the seven golden lampstands: "I know your works, your toil and your patient endurance. I know that you cannot tolerate evildoers; you have tested those who claim to be apostles but are not, and have found them to be false. I also know that you are enduring patiently and bearing up for the sake of my name, and that you have not grown weary. But I have this against you, that you have abandoned the love you had at first. Remember then from what you have fallen; repent, and do the works you did at first."

The church in Ephesus was consistent in its ministry. Jesus knew its works, its toil, and its patient endurance. It was functioning well as it endured patiently for the sake of Jesus' name, but there was something missing; the congregation had lost its first love of Jesus. Communities of Jesus' followers can perform the tasks of ministry but forget the outward focus of Jesus' call to discipleship. Rather than living in the missional identity of Jesus, their walk of discipleship can become mired in the inward focus of institutional functionality as they lose their vision (identity) by becoming focused on the functions of their ministry.

Communities of Jesus' followers can perform the tasks of ministry but forget the outward focus of Jesus' call to discipleship.

It is the intersecting of creative possibility and congregational focus that defines the four stages of congregational life. Whether a congregation is dealing with the demographics of a changing community, a change in congregational leadership, a change in congregational resources, or other changes, every local church will undergo the rhythm of organizational life stages that will affect its alignment with the mission of making disciples of Jesus Christ for the transformation of the world. This rhythm includes four congregational life stages:

Forming—The founding mission and vision of a congregation's existence is being defined. Creative possibility is embraced as a new community of Jesus' followers discerns and is shaped by an outward focus of mission.

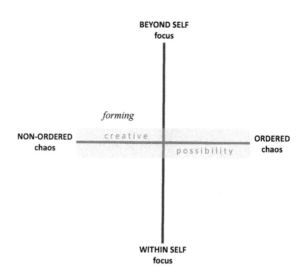

Aligning—The culture and resources of the congregation's institutional life is congruent with its mission and vision. The second stage of organizational life is defined by the need to balance the requirements of organizational structure with the established mission of organizational identity. The primary challenge in this phase of organizational existence is that organizational life tends to become settled in the comfortable expectations of known realities. In turn, expectations for the maintenance of organizational life can begin to drive the organization's reason for existence.

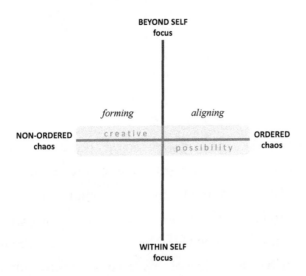

Forgetting—The internal needs of an organization outweigh its external vision. As the identity of a congregation becomes focused on maintaining its organizational existence, the missional reason for its existence can be forgotten. Its structures become rigid as it settles into known expectations of the present. Rather than existing as a movement of hope, its identity begins to be defined by discouragement.

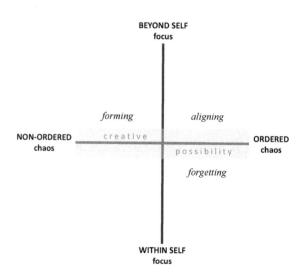

Wandering—The missional purpose is not being faithfully remembered as the outward focus of an organization is replaced by an inward focus that prompts the organization to forget the reason for its existence as it focuses its resources upon its survival rather than its mission. Amnesia best describes the reality of this stage, as a faith community is no longer defined by a clear missional reason for its existence. In this phase, chaos defines community existence. There is no alignment of ministries, as community life is destroyed by suspicion and accusations.

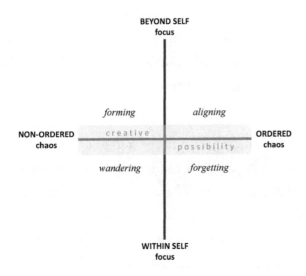

At any point in these life stages, the formation and reformation of congregational identity and ministry is possible, depending upon the priorities and behaviors of the congregation. Undergirded by the disciplines of faithful remembering, faithful equipping, and faithful encouraging, congregations are able to remain faithful to mission and vision that focuses beyond themselves. When congregations turn inward in their focus, the three disciplines of Christian transformation are replaced by the characteristics of inward institutional focus:

Wistful Wishing: A longing for past realities when the challenge of future possibilities is considered to be greater than present resources. Living in fear of an unknown future of vital creative possibilities, wistful wishing is clinging to known realities of the past, even when those realities produced less than desired results. Wistful wishing drags the congregation away from faithfully remembering the reason for its existence. An example of wistful wishing is found in Numbers 14:1-4 after the congregation of Israel received the report of the challenges that awaited them in the Promised Land by stating they wanted to return to the slavery of Egypt:

> Then all the congregation raised a loud cry, and the people wept that night. And all the Israelites complained against Moses and Aaron; the whole congregation said to them, "Would that we had died in the land of Egypt! Or would that we had died in this wilderness! Why is the LORD bringing us into this land to fall by the sword? Our wives and our little ones will become booty; would it not be better for us to go back to Egypt?" So they said to one another, "Let us choose a captain, and go back to Egypt."

An orchestra provides an example of an organization that cannot succeed when insular isolation exists. In an orchestra, each musician is talented with a particular instrument. If all musicians play their instrument spectacularly but to a different sheet of music, mayhem will ensue. Rather, the musical score has been written for the overall effect of a beautiful song. It has been adapted for each instrument. And the conductor leads the musicians as they play together for a successful outcome.

Insular Isolation: Inward focus identified by protective self-interest to the detriment of institutional well-being. The result of insular isolation is different organizational entities functioning with nonaligned objectives as they silo themselves in protective patterns of behavior. Rather than faithfully equipping congregational ministries by aligning resources toward vision, congregational resources are fragmented as the survival of specific ministries is emphasized.

Dispirited Discouragement: A lack of future hope expressed by the questioning of present organizational objectives and values that results from a fragmentation of vision and ministry. Dispirited discouragement results in a lack of personal commitment to the future vision of an organization as congregations begin to wander in search of meaning for their existence.

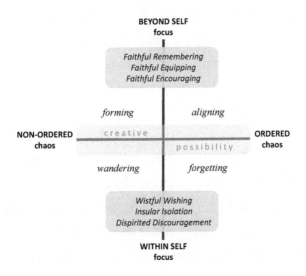

The good news is that vitality can be experienced in any of the stages of organizational life. Whether it is in the *forming stage* as vision is clearly defined; the *aligning stage,* where congregational resources and behavior are congruent with outward focus; *forgetting stage,* where institutional survival replaces outward vision; or *wandering stage,* where there is no clear vision, vitality can be experienced. What is required in any stage of congregational life are Christian transformational leaders who practice the disciplines of faithful remembering, faithful equipping, and faithful encouraging as they embrace the chaos of creative possibility by helping a congregation live in the servant identity of Jesus.

A Case in Point—Marc's Story

There have been many times I have heard the following statement, "This church needs to die before it can experience new life." My response to this statement is to invite conversation about what it means for Jesus' followers to follow their Savior into a new understanding of life.

Several of my pastoral appointments were to churches of varying sizes and locations where there had been declines in identified areas of congregational vitality such as worship and giving. At each of these churches, my ministry was guided by the disciplines of *faithful remembering, faithful equipping,* and *faithful encouraging. Faithful remembering* was practiced by having the congregation engage in a time of biblical reflection on what it means to be called to be disciples of Jesus. This discipline was experienced on both a corporate level through worship and teaching as well as individual conversations with congregational leaders and members. The goal of *faithful remembering* was to help the congregation turn its focus from concerns about survival to a vision of new life that is offered through Jesus' life, crucifixion, and resurrection.

Through the discipline of *faithful equipping*, congregational leaders became involved in an honest assessment of the congregation's current reality as members of the church were invited to talk about their hopes and concerns for the church and community. There were conversations with people in the community—with the goal of connecting the congregation and its neighbors. Demographic assessments were made of both the church and the community. The end result was an invitation for people to change the congregation's narrative from an inward focus to ministry defined by the servant identity of Jesus.

Faithful encouraging was practiced as congregational leaders made ministry choices that focused beyond present expectations. Language was shaped by the promise of God's future faithfulness rather than wistful wishing about the past.

—— Questions for Reflection and Discussion ——

1. How can congregational vitality be experienced in any life stage of a congregation?
2. Why should Christian transformational leaders embrace chaos?
3. How are the three disciplines of Christian transformational leadership different from wistful wishing, insular isolation, and dispirited discouragement?

CHAPTER FIVE

Lay Servants as Christian Transformational Leaders

Part One: The Ministry of Lay Servants

Certified lay servants tell the story of love for God and neighbor as they fulfill the disciplinary responsibilities of their ministry. They tell this story in partnership with pastors, district superintendents, and committees on lay servant ministries as they:

- provide leadership, assistance, and support to the program emphases of the church or other United Methodist ministry.
- lead meetings for prayer, training, study, and discussion.
- conduct, or assist in conducting, services of worship, preach the Word, or give addresses.
- work with appropriate committees and teams that provide congregational and community life or foster caring ministries.
- assist in the distribution of the elements of Holy Communion.
- teach the Scriptures, doctrine, organization, and ministries of The United Methodist Church.[1]

The ministries of local congregations and other United Methodist ministries are enriched through the work of lay servants. As noted in chapter three, the leadership of spiritually engaged laity is one of the four indicators of congregational vitality. For lay servants to be Christian transformational leaders, however, they must be willing to partner with fellow leaders in helping congregations and other United Methodist ministries to focus beyond current expectations.

——— Questions for Reflection and Discussion ———

1. How do lay servants tell the story of love for God and neighbor as they fulfill the disciplinary responsibilities of their ministry?
2. Why is the ministry of the lay servant a partnered ministry?
3. Are there ministries of the certified lay servant in which you have participated? Which of these ministries did you enjoy? Why did you enjoy these particular ministries?

Part Two: The Ministry of Christian Transformational Leaders

Christian transformational leaders tell the story of love for God and neighbor as they focus beyond current expectations by telling the story of creation in the present tense. They tell this story as their ministry is shaped by the four movements of creation that form the opening biblical creation account in Genesis 1:1-2:4a:

- Embracing Chaos
- Speaking Order to Creative Possibility

- Living in Sabbath Relationship
- The Ongoing Narrative of Creation

Movement One:
Genesis 1:1-2: Embracing Chaos

> In the beginning when God created the heavens and the earth, the earth was a formless void and darkness covered the face of the deep, while a wind from God swept over the face of the waters.

A prologue to the opening biblical story of creation, these first two verses of the Bible provide the foundation for the faith story of God's ongoing interaction with creation as revealed in the remaining verses of the Bible. To understand the creation account in the Bible, it is important to understand the identity of both God and chaos in creation.

The name by which God is identified in the prologue of this creation story is *Elohim*. A Hebrew word for God, *Elohim* shaped Israel's understanding of its relationship to the universal Creator of the heavens and the earth. A testimony of faith in the Creator's ordering presence, *Elohim* is the identity of God that is confessed in Deuteronomy 26:5-10 as the people of Israel are preparing to cross the Jordan River and enter the Promised Land after forty years of wandering in the wilderness. Realizing that the land on which they will live is a gift from God, they covenant to faithfully remember that God who spoke order to chaos in the beginning would speak order to the unknown realities they were about to encounter in the Promised Land.

The name by which chaos is identified in the prologue of the creation story is *tehom*.

A Hebrew word translated as "the deep" in Genesis 1:2, *tehom* refers to the primordial water over which the wind of God moved in Genesis 1:2. This verse, however, is not the only place in the Bible where *tehom* is identified. Genesis 7:11 states that *tehom* is one of the sources of water in the Great Flood in the days of Noah, and Isaiah 51:10 states that God dried up the waters of *tehom* so that Israel could walk on dry land through the sea in their Exodus from the slavery of Egypt.

It is both the identity of *Elohim* and the identity of *tehom* that set the stage for the Creator to speak order to chaos through the creation of the first six days of the week in Genesis 1:3-31. It is faith in both the creative power of God and the creative possibility of chaos that sets the stage for transformation as Christian transformational leaders embrace chaos.

God embraces and speaks order to chaos.

Movement Two
Genesis 1:3-31: Speaking Order to Creative Possibility

The second movement of the opening biblical story of creation is the creation of the first six days of the week in Genesis 1:3-31. Each day's creation begins with God speaking order to chaos with the phrase, "God said." Each day's creation account concludes with the result of God's ordering of creative possibility with the phrase "and there was." Framed within the structure of the first six days of the week being spoken into existence, Genesis 1:3-31 paints a portrait of creation as God embraces and speaks order to the essence of creative possibility that is found in chaos. While each day has a distinctive role in this creation account, the identity of each day cannot be understood fully outside of its interrelatedness with the other days of the week.

Christian transformational leaders understand that transformation is the ministry of ordering creative possibility. Like an artist with a palette of colors, these leaders paint a portrait of possibilities as they align resources with vision and mission. Understanding that God spoke order to creative possibility through the relationship of each day of the week, they speak order to creative possibility through the relationship of organizational realities with one another. Working in concert with fellow leaders and members of their congregations, they cast a vision beyond the present moment as they speak order to the present moment.

As God rested in the goodness of all that God had created, the purpose of creation was revealed: creation living in right relationship with the Creator.

Movement Three:
Genesis 2:1-3: Living in Sabbath Relationship

Thus the heavens and the earth were finished, and all their multitude. And on the seventh day God finished the work that he had done, and he rested on the seventh day from all the work that he had done. So God blessed the seventh day and hallowed it, because on it God rested from all the work that he had done in creation (Genesis 2:1-3).

Creation is understood through the Creator's blessing of the seventh day of the week. As God rested in the goodness of all that God created in the first six days of the week, the purpose of creation was revealed: creation living in right relationship with the Creator. Through the blessing of the seventh day, God created Sabbath relationship with all that God created in the first six days of the week. Unlike God's creative work in the first six days, however, God does not speak the seventh day into existence. Instead, God blesses the seventh day, as Sabbath points to the complete goodness of God's ordering of creative possibility. It is Sabbath that defines God's relationship with Israel in the Old Testament through the law ("Remember the Sabbath day, and keep it holy," Exodus 20:8) and the prophets (". . . if you call the sabbath a delight and the holy day of the LORD honorable," Isaiah 58:13b). Jesus used Sabbath to define his ministry ("For the Son of Man is lord of the sabbath," Matthew 12:8).

The desired result of Christian transformation is to live in the blessing of Sabbath relationship with God. The ministry of Christian transformational leaders is the story of creation being told in the present as these leaders embrace chaos, speak order to creative possibility, and witness to Sabbath relationship. Their ministry defines God's ongoing creative activity as witnessed in the concluding movement of the opening creation account of the Bible.

Movement Four:
Genesis 2:4a: The Ongoing Narrative of Creation

"These are the generations of the heavens and the earth when they were created."

Every generation is part of the ongoing story of God's creation. Living with faith in the presence of the Creator of heaven and earth, every generation tells the ongoing biblical story of faith as it seeks to live in right relationship with the Creator who embraces chaos, speaks order to creative possibility, and creates right relationship. The phrase that describes God's continuing interaction with every generation is *creatio continua*: "the continuation of God's work as Creator throughout the history of creation."[2] To live in right relationship with the Creator, every generation must acknowledge the ongoing creative power of God who still speaks order to the ongoing essence of creative possibility:

> Since chaos is not removed but controlled, God's activity in restraining chaos and sustaining order is a dimension of God's work in every generation. Whenever the order of things seems threatened and confusion or purposelessness reigns it is to trust in God's power as Creator, the source of order and meaning that the community of faith must turn.[3]

Christian transformational leaders realize the purpose of their ministry is to help the current generation of faith tell the story of right relationship that God created in the beginning.

A Case in Point—Marc's Story

When I was a pastor, the parents of a newborn child would often want to talk with me about whether their child should be baptized. In responding to their question, I would read Genesis 1:1-2 with them and review the baptismal liturgy of The United Methodist Church. As we talked, I would share with them about how the same Spirit of God that moved over the face of the deep would be moving over the water of their child's baptism. In turn, we would talk about how the ordering, creative presence of God would be part of their child's life as the story of their child's life was connected to the faith story of the biblical generations. We would talk about what it meant for them to live in Sabbath relationship with God, the church, each other, and their child as they raised their child in the faith of Jesus. Finally, we would review the vows of baptism and close with a prayer of thanksgiving for God's blessing of their family through the birth of their child.

This was one of the most sacred times I experienced as a pastor. It was a time of connecting, a time of blessing, a time of telling the story of creation in the present tense.

——— Questions for Reflection and Discussion ———

1. How is the ministry of the Christian transformational leader defined by the four movements of creation?
2. How have you seen the movements of creation demonstrated by Christian transformational leaders?

3. How do Christian transformational leaders help the current generation of faith tell the story of right relationship that God created in the beginning?

Part Three: The Identity Crisis of Church Leadership

Church leadership is facing an identity crisis. Questions about relevancy, mission, vision, right beliefs, right relationships, and survival require leaders who can be identified and trusted. In a chaotic whirlwind of cultural shifts and clashing values, Christian leaders are being called upon to define the reality in which twenty-first century congregations find themselves. Leading into this whirlwind, church leaders may wonder about the balancing act they must perform as they structure change with people who have divergent values that focus on the past, present, and future. It is in the context of these divergent values that Christian transformational leaders are identified as they tell the story of creation in the present tense. Embracing chaos, they speak order to creative possibility as they invite people to live in right relationship with the God of all generations.

Christian transformational leaders faithfully equip the current generation of Jesus' followers to witness to the right relationship that God makes possible through their Savior. Telling the story of *creatio continua*, they faithfully remember that the biblical story of faith is the narrative of God's ongoing creative activity as revealed through the life, death, and resurrection of Jesus.

He is the image of the invisible God, the first-born of all creation; for in him all things in heaven and on earth were created, things visible and invisible, whether thrones or dominions or rulers or powers—all things have been created through him and for him. He himself is before all things, and in him all things hold together. He is the head of the body, the church, he is the beginning, the firstborn from the dead, so that he might come to have first place in everything. For in him all the fullness of God was pleased to dwell, and through him God was pleased to reconcile to himself all things, whether on earth or in heaven, by making peace through the blood of his cross (Colossians 1:15-20).

A narrative of creation and reconciliation, the Bible tells a story of hope about the God of goodness who has spoken from the beginning and whose voice continues to be heard through Jesus. It is through this ongoing biblical story that every Christian community should understand its identity and its mission as it tells the story of God's hopefulness revealed through Jesus. By the power of this ongoing biblical story of faith, Christian transformational leaders are given the authority to speak order to chaos as they lead their faith communities and organizations into a future that is different from the past. Becoming part of a movement of hope that is defined by the power of God's goodness, they respond to present conditions through faith in Jesus. Embracing the ongoing biblical story of God's creative and redemptive power, they nurture followers of Jesus to live with faith in the hopeful, reconciling power of God's grace.

Christian transformational leaders realize the purpose of their ministry is to help their generation of faith tell the story of right relationship that God created in the beginning.

—— Questions for Reflection and Discussion ——

1. What is required for church leadership to be trusted?
2. How do Christian transformational leaders faithfully equip the current generation of Jesus' followers to witness to the right relationship that God makes possible through their Savior?
3. How is the biblical narrative of faith the ongoing story of God's creative activity as revealed through the life, death, and resurrection of Jesus?

Part Four: The Identity of Christian Transformational Leaders

Christian transformational leaders are identified by the ways they lead transformational change. With faith in the creative power of God and the creative possibility of chaos, they order creative possibility into future reality. Shaped by a calling to leadership that is undergirded through faith in the Creator, they influence change through a self-revealing vulnerability of faith in God rather than a self-proclaimed confidence in themselves. Understanding that transformational change cannot be forced upon the congregations they serve, they lead by focusing on the Sabbath relationship that God created in the beginning, redeemed through Jesus, and promised in the present and future through the Holy Spirit. Inviting people to join them in the journey of change, they emphasize the importance of a congregation's right relationship with God, with one another, and with their community. Rather than providing a checklist of tasks to be accomplished, they establish a framework for transforming relationships by asking these questions of right relationship as the prophet Micah, who asked:

> With what shall I come before the Lord, and bow myself before God on high? Shall I come before him with burnt offerings, with calves a year old? Will the Lord be pleased with thousands of rams, with ten thousands of rivers of oil? Shall I give my firstborn for my transgression, the fruit of my body for the sin of my soul? He has told you, O mortal, what is good; and what does the Lord require of you but to do justice, and to love kindness, and to walk humbly with your God? (Micah 6:6-8)

Christian transformational leaders influence change through a self-revealing vulnerability of faith in God rather than a self-proclaimed confidence in themselves.

In addition to asking right questions of the congregations they serve, Christian transformational leaders ask themselves how the identity of their leadership is shaping current reality. How much of their time is focused on envisioning a reality that is beyond the present? How much of their time is focused on maintaining the reality that is within the present? Are they expected to preserve the past that has led to the present? Are they called upon to protect the present and keep people satisfied in the moment? Will they have the boldness to claim spiritual authority by speaking to a future that is filled with faith and hope? How can they influence present opinion while leading beyond the present and, at the same time, influence future opinion while leading within the present?

A Case in Point—John's Story

Leading a church can be a difficult process because, over the years, most churches develop a leadership style that may or may not be effective in strengthening their mission. There are two fundamental requirements needed to develop an effective leadership team. First, leaders must recognize their role as disciples to be engaged in making disciples, and this recognition requires mature faith. Second, leaders must commit to the task of making disciples, regardless of their functional leadership position. Only a mature leadership team dedicated to the spiritual development of its members can move a congregation toward health and vitality.

Over the years, I have found that beginning a new year with a leadership retreat enables the leadership team to come together with a shared vision. Key leaders of the church council and I led these retreats. We focused first on the responsibility of being spiritual leaders and examples. Secondly, we focused on the responsibility of working as a unified presence toward meeting the mission of the church. Biblical teaching was the best basis for this. A favorite biblical story I told was the story of Esther, when Mordecai told Esther, "and who knows whether you have not come to the kingdom for such a time as this?" Leaders are called to serve, and they, too, are called to answer the question of whether they were born "for such a time as this."

These retreats were followed by ministry team meetings focused in a similar way, so that all discussions and decisions were founded in the holy purpose of making disciples of Jesus Christ for the transformation of the world.

Rather than providing answers that force change, Christian transformational leaders invite people to live into a new reality by asking questions of right focus for their congregations as well as themselves. Their questions of right focus are defined by the following realities of transformational leadership:

Transformational Leadership Reality One: It is the role of leaders to assess the current reality of creative possibility in an organization.

Transformational Leadership Reality Two: Leaders embrace chaos because they understand that creative possibility is present at all times in the life of an organization.

Transformational Leadership Reality Three: Leaders will either order creative possibility or chaos will disorder the essence of leadership.

Transformational Leadership Reality Four: It is the responsibility of leaders to identify, equip, and encourage relationships that can create a movement of hope.

Transformational Leadership Reality Five: The presence of chaos and the absence of transformational leadership means an organization will experience reality that is void of future vision.

Practicing the disciplines of faithful remembering, faithful equipping, and faithful encouraging (as detailed in chapter two), Christian transformational leaders can bring about transformational change. Understanding that God has the power to speak creative possibility into any situation, they realize that new life is possible at any stage of life (forming, aligning, forgetting, and wandering) in the organizations they lead.

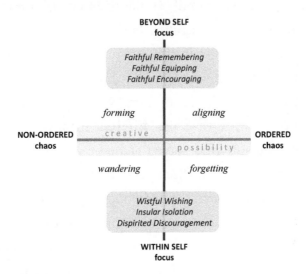

Transformational change tends to be associated with situations that are desperate and reeling: a church on the verge of closure or a business on the verge of collapse. We may think of congregations that have become disconnected from their communities and find themselves in the forgetting or wandering stages of organizational life. From the Bible, we might think of the story of the prodigal son in Luke 15 who asked for his share of the family inheritance, left home, squandered his property in dissolute living, wound up feeding pigs, was on the edge of starvation, and came back home with the hope that he might become one of his father's hired hands. As he was walking home, his father saw him and transformed the situation by running to his son, putting his arms around him, and kissing him. He then told his servants to bring out the best robe, put a ring on his son's finger and sandals on his feet, to kill the fatted calf, and to celebrate "for this son of mine was dead and is alive again; he was lost and is found!" (Luke 15:24.) It was a transformative moment: a movement of future hope.

There was another son in this story who was also in need of transformation: the son who stayed at home and was diligent in doing all that was requested of him. While his father rejoiced in the hope of a future that was different from the past for the prodigal son, the son who stayed at home could not rejoice as he told his father, "For all these years I have been working like a slave for you, and I have never disobeyed your command; yet you have never given me even a young goat so that I might celebrate with my friends. But when this son of yours came back, who has devoured your property with prostitutes; you killed the fatted calf for him!" (Luke 15:29-31.) He could not rejoice at the return of his prodigal brother because his vision was focused on the past.

Transformation is not only about situations that need to be turned around. Transformation is also about living beyond the comfort of known expectations that keep us from moving forward into the future. Transformation is witnessed when a congregation is able to focus beyond the comfort of its present expectations (especially when those expectations are meeting the benchmarks of success and faithfulness) as well as when it lives beyond wistful wishing about the past.

Transformational change can be experienced in any stage of organizational life. For this change to be experienced in a congregation, Christian transformational leaders are required to:

1. Demonstrate the practices of transformational leadership that are detailed in chapter one.
2. Practice the disciplines of Christian transformation described in chapter two.
3. Define congregational vitality and discern vital alignment as noted in chapter three.
4. Assess current reality as reviewed in chapter four.
5. Tell the story of creation in the present tense as shared in chapter five.

Transformation is witnessed when a congregation is able to focus beyond the comfort of its present expectations.

—— Questions for Reflection and Discussion ——

1. Why is church leadership facing an identity crisis?
2. What do you think is the current reality in which twenty-first-century congregations find themselves? How do the realities of Christian transformational leaders address this current reality?
3. How is the biblical story of faith the narrative of God's ongoing creative activity as revealed through the life, death, and resurrection of Jesus?

Part Five: Requirements of Christian Transformational Change

Transformational change is possible in any stage of organizational life. For this change to be experienced in a congregation, much is required of Christian transformational leaders. The following is a review of key principles from each chapter.

Chapter One: Demonstrate the practices of transformational leadership.

a. *Enduring Encouragement*—Christian transformational leaders who consistently remember, model, and encourage Jesus' teaching of servant leadership are required as they guide a congregation in aligning its current realities with transformed possibilities.

b. *Seeing Beyond Self-Focused Concerns*—For a congregation to live into the possibility of new realities, it must have the courage to follow Jesus, even when it means that congregation must take up its cross by embracing its present context. It is only when this happens that a congregation can follow Jesus into a new understanding of life that is made possible through the cross of Jesus and the empty tomb.

c. *Asking Right Questions*—Christian transformational leaders ask right questions that allow new conversations to occur. The focus of these questions is designed to allow space for the organization to engage in vulnerable conversations about value and desired identity.

d. *Leading by Having the Mind of Christ*—The goal of Christian transformational leaders is to allow the identity of Jesus to shape the identity of their leadership.

Chapter Two: Practice the disciplines of Christian transformation.

a. *Faithful Remembering*—A key component of faithful remembering is that God remembers us for who God created us to be. God also remembers us for who God loves and expects us to be as individuals, leaders, and as communities of faith. The goal of faithful remembering is to provide the foundation for Christian transformation that is aligned with God's will.

b. *Faithful Equipping*—The goal of faithful equipping is to help people align their lives with Jesus' call to discipleship. The desired outcome of faithful equipping is a community of faithful disciples who will seek to answer God's call upon their lives and the life of their congregation.

c. *Faithful Encouraging*—Followers of Jesus believe the Holy Spirit empowers fullness of life through Jesus. It is the ministry of a Christian transformational leader to faithfully encourage people to live with enduring faith in Jesus.

Chapter Three: Define congregational vitality and discern vital alignment.

a. *Defining Congregational Vitality*—Congregations are vital when they are aligned toward the vision of life that God has cast through Jesus.

b. *Discerning Vital Alignment*—Determining whether a congregation's efforts are moving in the direction of its mission.

    i.   What must we KEEP doing to accomplish our mission?

    ii. What must we STOP doing that is not aligned with our mission?

    iii. What must we START doing to achieve our mission?

Chapter Four: Define and assess current reality and congregational life stage.

a. *Defining Current Reality*—A compilation of past realities and future possibilities through which the congregational culture intersects with the community culture.

b. *Assessing Current Reality*—Christian transformational leaders review how congregational values, resources, and behaviors align with the prayer that Jesus taught.

c. *Congregational Life Stages*—Congregational life stages may be understood as the intersection of chaos and focus. One of the basic roles of Christian transformational leadership is to bring some sort of order to organizational chaos in whatever life stage a congregation finds itself: forming, aligning, forgetting, or wandering.

Chapter Five: Tell the story of creation in the present tense.

Christian transformational leaders understand that transformation is the ministry of ordering creative possibility as they embrace and speak order to creative possibility by witnessing to Sabbath relationship with God.

A tool that can assist Christian transformational leaders in fulfilling their responsibilities is the "Model for Organizational Effectiveness." This simple model shows the order and relationship of factors that can lead to congregational vitality. Organizations that are intentional about these factors can successfully align themselves for maximum impact. Christian transformational leaders understand that congregations must organize themselves to be good stewards of the gifts God has given them. This model offers a logical order for thinking through these important factors.

MODEL FOR
ORGANIZATIONAL EFFECTIVENESS

The mission of The United Methodist Church is clear: to make disciples of Jesus Christ for the transformation of the world. This is the reason The United Methodist Church exists. Each congregation is unique in how it responds to this mission. There is not a one-size-fits-all approach to vitality. Every congregation has its own history, setting, gifts, strengths, challenges, and dreams. God has orchestrated these realities into a holy calling specific to each congregation.

In responding to God's holy calling, a congregation must answer the question: "What are we called to do because of why we exist?" Entering into a time of prayerful discernment, congregations must pray about what this question means for their future as they ponder "Why did God put us in this place, at this time, with these gifts?"

Once the vision (WHY) and the mission (WHAT) are clear, only then can a congregation effectively determine the right organizational structure (HOW), the right people (WHO), and the budget (COST) needed to fulfill God's calling. Key to understanding the "Model for Organizational Effectiveness" is the progression from a congregation's strategic questions of WHY and WHAT to the tactical implementation of HOW, WHO, and COST. Many congregations begin with asking tactical questions of HOW, WHO, and COST rather than strategic questions of WHY and WHAT. Classic stories about churches quarrelling over the color of carpet are examples of churches becoming stuck in the tactics of ministry rather than discerning a strategic vision of ministry. Rather than arguing about the color of carpet, congregations should more appropriately ask what role the carpet and facility have in the fulfillment of their vision and mission.

To avoid this snare, the results of a congregation's ministry should be measured by developing its own metrics of vitality. Congregations can measure vitality in many ways. To do this, they must answer the simple question, "What are signs that will indicate whether we are standing still, moving backward, or making progress?"

In the "Model for Organizational Effectiveness," the question of vitality is the measurement by which all ministries are evaluated. Every congregation should periodically work through a discernment model such as this to be intentional about how it is responding to its vision and mission.

A Case in Point—Kathy's Story

As an executive in the business world, I was constantly working through a model like this. We assumed nothing as a "given." Vision could be changed, mission could be adjusted, organizational structures could be redesigned, people could be more appropriately matched to the new structure, and budgets could be developed to finance the new plans. Once metrics of success were discerned and put into place, we were able to determine our progress toward our mission. When we made significant progress, we adjusted to our new reality and did it all over again. We were constantly intentional about these factors for organizational effectiveness as we produced our desired outcomes and moved the company forward.

In my work as a consultant with churches, it sometimes seems that church leaders take too much as a "given." The only parts of the model that are God-given are the vision of making disciples and the unique setting and gifts of each congregation. The rest of the plan is up to the leaders of the congregation. Bringing order to the chaos of the organization is the role of Christian transformational leaders.

An example of this occurred when I was working with a church regarding a new ministry that they thought would connect them to their community. They determined that even though it was a good idea, it was impossible to move forward because they "had no money." As the conversation developed, I realized that they actually had an annual budget of $900,000. That's A LOT of money! But, they were unconsciously choosing to spend the money on what they had always spent it on rather than reexamining their plans for relevancy and alignment. Surely there were things they could stop doing in order to finance this new, important ministry.

Each component of the "Model for Organizational Effectiveness" involves church leaders understanding what is a given and what is open to change. It is never easy to change an organizational structure, the roles people play, or to raise more money to fund a new approach. But it's much more possible when those plans are connected to a well-understood and well-stated holy vision and mission.

—— **Questions for Reflection and Discussion** ——

1. Which of the key principles of Christian transformational leadership do you find most satisfying in your ministry? Which of the key principles do you find most challenging?
2. Why is it important to begin with strategic questions, rather than tactical questions, about your congregation's ministry?
3. What are some signs that indicate whether congregations are standing still, moving backward, or making progress in vitality?

Part Six: Lay Servants as Christian Transformational Leaders

The ministry of lay servants as Christian transformational leaders is required if The United Methodist Church is going to fulfill its mission of making disciples of Jesus Christ for the transformation of the world. Grounding their ministry in the foundation of Jesus' call to love God and neighbor, lay servants as Christian transformational leaders are essential for the transformation of local congregations, workplaces, and the world.

As they live out their calling, lay servants as Christian transformational leaders are like the prophet Jeremiah called by God to go to the potter's house. As Jeremiah watched the potter work and rework clay into a useful vessel, he heard a message about God's ongoing creative and redemptive activity.

> The word that came to Jeremiah from the Lord: "Come, go down to the potter's house, and there I will let you hear my words." So I went down to the potter's house, and there he was working at his wheel. The vessel he was making of clay was spoiled in the potter's hand, and he reworked it into another vessel, as seemed good to him. Then the word of the Lord came to me: "Can I not do with you, O house of Israel, just as the potter has done? says the Lord. Just like the clay in the potter's hand, so are you in my hand, O house of Israel" (Jeremiah 18:1-6).

The story of the potter is a powerful illustration of God's active engagement in the work of creation and transformation. Just as God shaped and reshaped the house of Israel, God shapes and reshapes today's church into a vessel that "seems good to him."

Like Jeremiah who shared the story of how Israel was clay in God's hands, Christian transformational leaders share the story of how the church is clay in God's hands. Their leadership tells the story of God's ongoing creation and redemption as they actively engage in God's shaping and reshaping of their congregations. They lead their communities of faith to become vital congregations of disciples who follow Jesus by loving God and neighbor.

Placed in a unique area of influence, they are a consistent and constant voice within the life of a congregation. While pastors are appointed for a season, lay servants often serve during the seasons of several, perhaps many, pastors' ministries. Realizing that pastors have the disciplinary responsibility of ordering the ministry of a congregation, lay servants as Christian transformational leaders stand beside and with clergy and other congregational leaders in shaping the culture of a congregation.

They witness to the power of God by helping congregations embrace chaos, speak order to creative possibility, live in Sabbath relationship, and witness to the ongoing narrative of creation. It is in these times that lay servants as *Christian transformational leaders* must remember the lesson of the potter as they fulfill the disciplinary responsibilities of their ministry—the ministry of a lay servant as a Christian transformational leader. Is God calling you to the potter house?

—— **Questions for Reflection and Discussion** ——

1. How does the ministry of lay servants as Christian transformational leaders witness to holy expectations?
2. Why are the ministries of lay servants as Christian transformational leaders essential for vital congregations?
3. How do lay servants as Christian transformational leaders tell the story of creation in the present tense as they fulfill the disciplinary responsibilities of their ministry?

NOTES

Chapter One

1. ¶120 *The Book of Discipline of The United Methodist Church–2016* (Nashville, TN: The United Methodist Publishing House, 2016), 93.

Chapter Two

1. "On Love," *The Works of John Wesley, Third Edition, Complete and Unabridged, Volume 7* (Grand Rapids, Baker Book House Company, 1996), 495.
2. "Salvation by Faith," *The Works of John Wesley, Third Edition, Complete and Unabridged, Volume 5* (Grand Rapids, Baker Book House Company, 1996), 15.
3. *The Works of John Wesley, Volume 5*, 9.
4. *The Works of John Wesley, Third Edition, Complete and Unabridged, Volume 1* (Grand Rapids, Baker Book House Company, 1996), 103.

Chapter Three

1. ¶120 *The Book of Discipline of The United Methodist Church–2008* (Nashville, TN: The United Methodist Publishing House, 2008), 87.
2. ¶120 *The Book of Discipline–2008*, 87.
3. Call to Action Steering Team, http://umccalltoaction.org, 7.
4. ¶138, *The Book of Discipline of The United Methodist Church–2016* (The United Methodist Publishing House: Nashville, TN 2016), 100.
5. ¶255.2, *The Book of Discipline–2016*, 215.
6. ¶255.2a-f, *The Book of Discipline–2016*, 215-216.

Chapter Four

1. Marc Brown, Kathy Merry, John Briggs, *Does Your Church Have a Prayer? In Mission Toward the Promised Land: Participant's Workbook* (Nashville: Discipleship Resources), 2013, 23.
2. Marc Brown, Kathy Merry, and John Briggs, "Becoming a Tribe of Remembering Encouragers," *Leading Ideas* (Lewis Center for Church Leaders), November 4, 2009, https://www.churchleadership.com/leading-ideas/becoming-a-tribe-of-remembering-encouragers.

Chapter Five

1. ¶266.2, *The Book of Discipline of The United Methodist Church–2016* (Nashville, TN: The United Methodist Publishing House, 2016), 215-216.
2. Bruce C. Birch, *Let Justice Roll Down: The Old Testament, Ethics, and Christian Life* (Louisville, Kentucky Westminster/John Knox Press, 1991), 76.
3. Bruce C. Birch, 76.

CPSIA information can be obtained
at www.ICGtesting.com
Printed in the USA
LVHW021944200219
608188LV00008B/10/P